All That
God Cares
About

All That God Cares About

Common Grace and Divine Delight

Richard J. Mouw

Brazos Press

a division of Baker Publishing Group
Grand Rapids, Michigan

© 2020 by Richard J. Mouw

Published by Brazos Press
a division of Baker Publishing Group
PO Box 6287, Grand Rapids, MI 49516-6287
www.brazospress.com

Printed in the United States of America

Library of Congress Cataloging-in-Publication Data
Names: Mouw, Richard J., author.
Title: All that God cares about : common grace and divine delight / Richard J. Mouw.
Description: Grand Rapids, MI : Brazos Press, a division of Baker Publishing Group, 2020. | Includes bibliographical references.
Identifiers: LCCN 2019040929 | ISBN 9781587434754 (paperback)
Subjects: LCSH: Grace (Theology)
Classification: LCC BT761.3 .M677 2020 | DDC 234—dc23
LC record available at https://lccn.loc.gov/2019040929

ISBN: 978-1-58743-494-5 (casebound)

20   21   22   23   24   25   26   7   6   5   4   3   2   1

In keeping with biblical principles of creation stewardship, Baker Publishing Group advocates the responsible use of our natural resources. As a member of the Green Press Initiative, our company uses recycled paper when possible. The text paper of this book is composed in part of post-consumer waste.

With love to Dirk Mouw:
son, friend, and—increasingly
over the years—my teacher

Contents

Contents

Acknowledgments

In writing this book I have drawn from some materials that I presented at conferences during the past decade. I also make some use of two major lectures I delivered in the Netherlands: the 2015 Kuyper Lecture at the Vrije Universiteit and, in that same year, the first annual Bavinck Lecture at the Theologische Universiteit Kampen.

> The 2015 Kuyper Lecture at the Vrije Universiteit in Amsterdam was published as "Of Pagan Festivals and Metanarratives: Recovering the Awareness of Our Shared Humanness," *The Scottish Journal of Theology* 60, no. 3 (2017): 251–63.

> The 2015 Bavinck Lecture, "Neo-Calvinism: A Theology for the Global Church in the 21st Century," is posted online at https://en.tukampen.nl/portal-informatiepagina /herman-bavinck-lecture-richard-mouw-2.

I also draw at some points on material from these two published articles:

"The Bible and Cultural Discipleship," *Comment* 30, no. 2 (Fall 2012): 23–29.

"'In Him All Things Hold Together': Why God Cares about Ancient Chinese Vases," *Crux* 49, no. 3 (Fall 2013): 2–10.

I am grateful to have received permission to revisit my reflections from these earlier works.

Introduction

One of my favorite Italian words is *aggiornamento*—pronounced "ah-jyor-na-*men*-to." My saying that, of course, does not really amount to much. Since I am not a speaker or reader of Italian, it is not as if I have chosen that word as my favorite from hundreds of others that I know.

In my youth I went to public schools with some highly intelligent Italian-American kids, but I am pretty sure that I never heard one of them ever utter the word *aggiornamento*. I was introduced to that word in the early 1960s, as I followed with interest the reports coming from Rome about the Second Vatican Council. During the three years that Vatican II met, there was a lot of talk about *aggiornamento*. The word means "updating," and that was what was happening as the bishops met in Rome. They made important changes to revitalize Catholic thought and practice for the late twentieth century.

This book is my attempt to contribute to what I see as a much-needed neo-Calvinist *aggiornamento*. My effort here focuses specifically on an updating of the doctrine of common grace as it was set forth by Abraham Kuyper in the Netherlands in the last half of the nineteenth century.

1

I will also be doing a bit of personal *aggiornamento* in these pages. When I was invited to give the 2000 Stob Lectures, I immediately decided upon common grace as my topic. In preparing those lectures, I reviewed some of the debates—church-dividing ones—that had taken place during the first half of the twentieth century among North American Dutch Calvinists. When my lectures appeared in book form, though, I was pleasantly surprised by some positive interest from beyond the Reformed community. The comments and questions I received stimulated some new thoughts on the subject.

The new thoughts were further enhanced and multiplied by what I have been learning from my PhD students at Fuller Seminary, especially since I have been able to devote more time to doctoral mentoring after retiring in 2013 from a twenty-year stint as the seminary's president and becoming a full-time faculty member again. As I am writing this book, ten of my students have successfully defended dissertations on neo-Calvinist topics, with a half dozen more making excellent progress. The majority of these students have been attracted to the thought of Abraham Kuyper and Herman Bavinck from non-Reformed backgrounds, and their enthusiasm for the subject matter and their fresh insights have provided me with an ongoing neo-Calvinist education.

But my *aggiornamento* interests also have a broader focus. I am convinced that the neo-Calvinist perspective speaks in profound ways to our present cultural situation in North America. In my own personal theological-spiritual journey I have always described my identity as both "Calvinist" and "evangelical." I still claim both labels. And while the latter term has come into some disrepute in recent decades because of the way it has come to be associated with a mean-spirited "politicizing," I am convinced that some of the defects associated with this reputation can be remedied by drawing upon an updated—a recontextualized—neo-Calvinism.

Protection versus Engagement

Abraham Kuyper himself would have liked the idea that his theological insights needed to be updated in the light of new cultural realities. Indeed, it is precisely this *aggiornamento* character of Kuyper's thought that motivates many of us to call ourselves *neo*-Calvinists. Kuyper disagreed with John Calvin on some important points, especially relating to the Reformer's views on church-state relations, and this led Kuyper to expand on basic Calvinist ideas in articulating his theology of cultural engagement.

When he visited Princeton Seminary in 1898 to deliver the Stone Lectures, Kuyper introduced his perspective on the relevance of Calvinist theology to contemporary life by informing his audience that he had not come "to restore [Calvinism to] its worn-out form," but rather to address the basic principles of Calvinism in a way that meets "the requirements of our own century."[1] In offering that assessment, Kuyper was signaling his enthusiasm for updating Calvinism—even revising it at some key points—as the Calvinist movement faced new cultural realities.

This statement of purpose contrasted in a stark manner to remarks that had been made at Princeton twenty-six years earlier by the great theologian Charles Hodge, when on April 24, 1872, he addressed over five hundred people who had gathered to honor him for fifty years of his scholarship and teaching at Princeton Seminary. In those comments, Hodge articulated what a recent biographer describes as "the defining, oracular statement of his life." What he was especially proud of, Hodge declared, was that during his half century of service at Princeton "a new idea never originated in this Seminary."[2]

To be sure, these quite different expressions of what it means to be faithful to the Reformed tradition are not fully

3

accurate measures of how Hodge and Kuyper actually went about their respective theological tasks. Hodge was obviously capable of breaking new ground. And Kuyper could certainly resist new theological thoughts, as he frequently did in some of the ecclesiastical controversies in which he was actively engaged.

Nonetheless, the two expressions represent, in the abstract at least, differing dominant tendencies within the broad tradition of Reformed orthodoxy. One tendency is *theological protectionism*, a posture of resistance to significant theological innovation, while the other is what we can label *creative engagement* with new cultural realities.

While both of these tendencies are meant to serve the cause of Calvinist orthodoxy, there has long been disagreement within the Reformed tradition regarding what exactly is required by way of faithful subscription to the Reformed confessions. Some have insisted on "line-by-line" assent to each mode of formulation in each confessional document, while others have stipulated that sincere assent be given to the basic theological *principles* affirmed by those documents. But in neither case has it been acceptable for a person to claim confessional fidelity and disagree with the details of what is clearly *taught* in the confessions. Within those boundaries, then, Hodge and Kuyper would have seen each other as obvious co-defenders of Reformed orthodoxy.

My own theological sympathies are firmly on the Kuyperian side of the spectrum. We live in a time of rapid change—both in the larger cultures in which we spend our daily lives and also in our efforts to support the ongoing mission of the Christian community in the midst of that cultural change. The challenges are great, but I like to see them as providential opportunities to present the message of the gospel in a manner that is appropriate to the times and cultural contexts in which the church finds itself.

The Scope

My primary purpose in this book is to clarify some of the basic themes of the neo-Calvinist perspective on common grace—along with the larger account that Kuyper offered of God's intentions for cultural development in the context of the overall pattern of the biblical narrative.

In pursuing my purpose here, I will not be providing a general introduction to neo-Calvinism. That kind of overview is available elsewhere—most notably in Al Wolters's *Creation Regained*[3] and, more recently, Craig Bartholomew's *Contours of the Kuyperian Tradition*.[4]

And, even in focusing specifically on common grace, I won't be attempting to provide a detailed exposition of the theological debates that have shaped the development of the common-grace doctrine over the past century and a half. Fortunately, that kind of detailed discussion has recently become accessible in English with the publication of Jochem Douma's 1966 Dutch dissertation that focuses on a hundred years of neo-Calvinist treatments of common grace.[5] I learned much from reading this careful—and painstakingly detailed—study. For the complex narrative of neo-Calvinist discussions of common grace in particular, Douma's book is surely now the authoritative guide. My purpose here is to explore primarily those themes that have direct relevance to our contemporary appropriation of common-grace teachings.

1

God's Complex Concerns

My motivation for writing this book got a boost when someone told me a story about Abraham Kuyper's nightly spiritual ritual. I think I had heard or read the story before, but this time it hit me a little differently. It was about Kuyper facing the crucifix on the wall of his bedroom every evening and speaking to the Savior. Before lying down on his bed each night, Kuyper reported, he would look up to the cross and confess that he had not done enough that day to share in Christ's suffering.

The person who told me that story considered it to be spiritually edifying, and it did have that immediate effect on me. It still does. But the more I thought about it, I also experienced a little bit of spiritual—and theological—uneasiness. Given everything I know and like about Kuyper's theology, the story is a bit of a puzzler. Did he really end every day with a sense of regret about his failure to suffer adequately? Weren't there some days where he simply reported some upbeat thoughts and feelings to the Savior?

Here is a scenario I have toyed with. Imagine Kuyper looking up at Jesus on the cross and telling him what a great afternoon he had spent at one of the fine Dutch art museums. "It was delightful, Lord," he would say. "I especially enjoyed some of the nineteenth-century landscapes. I am so grateful that you created a world in which it is possible to spend several hours appreciating that kind of art!" Or maybe on some days he could tell Jesus about an exciting soccer match he had attended. Or he could describe the enjoyable time he had spent at the dinner table with his family.

I would be surprised if Kuyper did not actually end some of his days telling Jesus about the positive things. He believed that God has not given up on the creation. God's good purposes for the world have not been canceled because of our rebellion. Someday Christ will return to make all things new. To get ready for that glorious future, we need to discern the signs of God's renewing work in the present, looking for the gifts that the Lord wants us to enjoy as we make our way through the complex cultural realities that surround us.

But we do still need to be constantly reminded about Christ's call to us to share in his suffering. The ravages of the fall are all too obvious in our world, and simply to ignore them or to avoid participating in the pain that afflicts the human condition is to be disobedient to the demands of the gospel.

Those Desolate Square Inches

Two framed photos sit side by side on a shelf in my office at Fuller Seminary, one of Abraham Kuyper and the other of Dorothy Day. I got the idea from Dirk Jellema, who was a history professor at Calvin College when I joined the faculty there in the late 1960s. He had photos of the two of them on the wall in his office. When I moved to Fuller Seminary in 1985, I did the same in my new office.

I never asked Dirk why he paired Kuyper's picture with that of the American-born founder of the network of Catholic Worker houses. After encountering Christ and converting to Catholicism in the 1920s, Dorothy Day devoted herself to peacemaking activities and lived among the poor, serving them with food and shelter on a daily basis. This was a far cry from Kuyper's role as the founder of a university and a national leader in Dutch politics. I have always assumed, though, that Dirk saw Day as providing a necessary supplement to Kuyper's socioeconomic thought.

I wrote about the need for a supplement of that sort in my book *Uncommon Decency: Christian Civility in an Uncivil World*. But because I figured that contemporary readers would be more familiar with Mother Teresa than with Dorothy Day, I titled one of my chapters, "Abraham Kuyper, Meet Mother Teresa."[1]

In that chapter I pointed out that when Kuyper referred to Jesus—which he did quite often—he seemed to be especially fond of depicting the ascended Christ. His well-known manifesto about Jesus ruling over every square inch of the creation is an obvious case in point. That is not a christological emphasis that showed up in Mother Teresa's talk about Jesus. She was all about finding Jesus among the poorest of the poor, with a special emphasis on those whom she served in India—dying lepers on the streets of Calcutta.

In my chapter on Kuyper and Mother Teresa, I warned against a triumphalist tendency in Kuyperian thought. Jesus has indeed redeemed the whole creation from the curse of our fallenness, and our task as followers of Christ is to go out to those square inches and reclaim them for the cause of the kingdom. But this may often mean committing ourselves to suffer alongside those who live in desperate situations. A good corrective, I argued, is to hear the call to identify with the concerns of Jesus that Mother Teresa took so seriously, following him to those lonely square inches on the margins of society: among the homeless, the abused, the dying lepers, the victims of injustice.

In preparing a lecture on Kuyper's social thought, I went very carefully through an address that he gave in 1891 to the first Christian Social Congress in the Netherlands, a large gathering of Calvinists engaged in bringing a Christian witness to the labor movement. While there is a good English version of that speech published as a small book translated by James Skillen, *The Problem of Poverty*, I continue to use my well-marked-up version of Dirk Jellema's earlier translation, published by him with the title *Christianity and the Class Struggle*.

In my recent rereading of Kuyper's speech, I discovered more of Dorothy Day and Mother Teresa in what Kuyper said than I remembered seeing before. "When rich and poor stand opposed to each other," Kuyper told his audience, the Savior "never takes His place with the wealthier, but always stands with the poorer. . . . Powerful is the trait of pity, which is imprinted on every page of the Gospel where Jesus comes in contact with the suffering and oppressed." Jesus, who is himself the Bread of Life, Kuyper observed, also takes ordinary bread very seriously. In ministering to a hungry crowd, "He breaks the loaf into many pieces and gives them an abundance of precious fish." And then Kuyper made this remark, which suggests that he likely would have felt a special attraction to the twentieth-century ministry of Mother Teresa to dying lepers in Calcutta: Jesus, Kuyper told his 1891 audience, "does not hold back His hand from the touch of leprous flesh."[2]

I still wish that Kuyper could have met Mother Teresa and Dorothy Day. But having discovered this reference by him to the way Jesus ministered to lepers, I am now confident that he would have warmly greeted the two women—as I am sure he already has, in the direct presence of the Savior whom the three of them loved and served during their earthly journeys.

Many "Faces"

I tell all of that to emphasize that I care deeply about a neo-Calvinism that takes suffering seriously. We do not need less of an awareness of Christ's call to share in the sufferings of the world. But we do need to hear the call to take delight in God's present gifts.

I once heard a lecture by Neil Postman, who was a well-known critic of the mass media. In his talk he used the kind of example that would be familiar to readers of his 1985 *Amusing Ourselves to Death*. You meet an old friend on the street and, having not seen him for a while, ask him how his life has been going. "Well," he says, "my daughter got accepted at Cornell last month, and recently I bought a new car, a Honda. I really enjoyed seeing the Dodgers play the Cardinals, and last night my wife died of a heart attack. And speaking of my wife, she and I had a great meal a week ago at a new French restaurant."

That may come across as a very strange report, Postman said, but it is exactly the sort of thing that happens on the nightly news. We get a bulletin about an earthquake in Chile, then a report about a congressional vote on a tax bill. Then something about the murder rate in Chicago followed by a funny thing that happened to a high school student in Nebraska. And then: "When we get back from a brief break, our weather report."

His point was that the media report brief snippets about many different events: routine, tragic, entertaining, informative—all delivered in sequence without any attention to the unique character of each of the events being reported. And we viewers take it all in stride.

I heard Postman give that talk at a luncheon during a consultation of theological educators. It so happened that in the hours before we broke for lunch we had been discussing the curricular challenges in educating people for the increasingly complex tasks in church ministries. Hearing what Postman obviously meant as a negative critique of television newscasts, it struck me that the pattern he was criticizing was not unrelated to ministry complexities.

A pastor once told me about a difficult day he had just experienced. In the morning he visited a couple who had just brought their newborn—a healthy girl—home from the hospital and wanted the pastor to offer a prayer of blessing on their newly expanded family. From there he visited a woman whose husband had just died of cancer. Then he met with staff members about a budget shortfall, after which he joined the youth group for a pizza supper. That evening he and his wife watched *Jeopardy*.

He had to present different "faces" that day: happiness for the new parents, grief for the new widow, serious wrestling over staff financial concerns, "fun" with the youth group, leisure time as a husband.

This is not to defend television news programs against Neil Postman's critique. The media can do much better in reporting about the complexities of what goes on in the world. But it is to say that the challenges that arise in reporting the news are not unlike what a pastor faces in a day of active ministry. Indeed, they are faced by all of us who care deeply about what touches the heart of God. The One who "does not hold back His hand from the touch of leprous flesh" has also designed his creation in such a way that we can enjoy afternoons at art museums.

2

The Joys of Discipleship

The uneasiness that I experienced when I heard the story of Abraham Kuyper and his crucifix was reinforced a while later when a group of us—all theologians—spent an hour or so discussing the idea of discipleship. Dietrich Bonhoeffer's classic book on the subject, *The Cost of Discipleship*, came up early on, and "cost" became a prominent motif in what people had to say. To follow Jesus is for each of us to take up our own cross. We must give our all for the sake of the gospel, without thinking about what makes us happy. There may come times in our journeys when we must willingly accept persecution, and even death, out of obedience to Christ. People used language about the "cruciform" structure of the Christian life, and someone cited Søren Kierkegaard's insistence that it is not so much that "the way is narrow" but that "the narrowness is the way."[1]

Fair enough. Who can argue with any of that? I have given many class lectures criticizing the ethics of "self-actualization," and I have done my fair share of talking about the need to submit to the radical claims of the gospel. While I have typically failed to live up to my own preaching on these, I have never intentionally downplayed the role of suffering in the Christian life.

Still, I have often been troubled by portrayals of discipleship that make it *all* about suffering. Here, for example, is John Howard Yoder on what it means to imitate Christ: "Only at one point," he writes, "only on one subject—but then consistently and universally—is Jesus our example: in his cross."[2] Really? I want to ask. Consistently and universally? For one thing, at least some important dimensions of what Jesus went through on the cross were meant to make it unnecessary for us to do what he did on Calvary. Those dimensions—thank God—are unimitable. They were accomplished "in our place."

But my Reformed theology makes me want to look more broadly than simply at the cross, at the kind of life Jesus lived on the *way to* the cross. He came to fulfill the law, living a life in his humanity of perfect obedience to the will of God. He honored his parents. He loved his neighbor. He enjoyed things without coveting what others possessed. He apparently took great satisfaction from curing a Roman soldier's grief by raising the man's daughter from the dead. He acted decisively when no one had thought to plan for a meal at a gathering of thousands of people.

To be sure, I know what Yoder was wanting to avoid in his emphasis on our imitating the suffering of the cross. Without some serious theological focus, a "What would Jesus do?" ethic can be silly, if not dangerous. What would Jesus do if, for example, he was on an island without a boat and wanted to get to the mainland? We know the answer, but we had better not try to imitate him!

14

Costs and Benefits

Yoder was right to encourage us to place some theological limits on what it means to imitate Jesus. But, from my Reformed perspective, he made the limits too narrow.

I came away from that particular theological discussion of discipleship, then, with a commitment to trying to get clearer about not only the "costs" but also the present "benefits" of discipleship. And I want to emphasize the word "present." No one who puts a strong emphasis on the suffering dimensions of the Christian life denies the promise of a future happiness for all who walk the path of discipleship on this earthly journey. "I consider that our present sufferings are not worth comparing with the glory that will be revealed in us" (Rom. 8:18 NIV).

Is it simply all delayed satisfaction, though? Do we concentrate on suffering in the here and now in anticipation of a glory that will someday be revealed?

Actually, I don't think that the theologians who participated in that discussion of discipleship really had such a stark view of the Christian life. I heard one of them, for example, telling a colleague how much he enjoyed seeing the Dodgers win with a three-run homer in the ninth inning the night before. And another of the theologians had said, in a conversation just before the formal discussion began, that she and her husband had just had a wonderful time with their grandchildren. From the smile on her face I am certain she saw that family time as one of the blessings of the Christian life—as something that Jesus approved of, even though it involved no obvious suffering.

The problem, however, is that we tend not to think of such things when we start talking about discipleship. At least this is my impression. When we discuss discipleship, our tone gets serious, and seriousness for us often carries connotations of suffering.

Later, I tried my hunch on this out with a few of my theologian friends. I told them that someone has used an illustration of a well-known Christian leader who had a crucifix on the wall above his bed, and he testified that each evening when he was ready to slip into bed he looked up at the crucifix and asked the Lord to forgive him for the ways he failed to participate fully in the Savior's sufferings that day. Then I asked my friends whether they thought it might be acceptable for him on a particular occasion also to look up to the crucifix and say: "Jesus, thank you for saving me! Today I had a wonderful day of discipleship. I took my grandchildren to Disneyland and we had a great time together!"

My friends first had puzzled looks on their faces, but then they agreed that there was nothing really theologically objectionable in saying that to Jesus. The pause between puzzlement and approval, though, was significant for me.

Help from Bonhoeffer

My nagging concerns on this subject motivated me to go back once again to Bonhoeffer's classic discussion. I was hoping he could at least give me a word of encouragement in getting beyond the rather consistent emphasis on suffering. And I did not have to go very far into his discussion to find what I was looking for. Bonhoeffer does rather quickly get into talk about the "yoke" of Jesus, pointing us to a way that "is hard, unutterably hard, for those who try to resist it." But for those who submit to Jesus we experience the "kindly yoke" that we bear as disciples, even as we must stay aware of "the seriousness of his commands."[3]

More significantly, he sets up the "kindly yoke" theme with a reference to joy just four pages into his introduction. Because we walk "a road of boundless mercy" as we follow Jesus, says

Bonhoeffer, we can also proclaim this: "Discipleship means joy."[4]

Bonhoeffer returns to the idea of joy near the end of his book, when he emphasizes that "the Christian life is not one of gloom, but of ever increasing joy in the Lord." There is some hiddenness about the grounding of this joy, "for in the present all we know is his good work."[5] So we await a future revealing of the glory.

Given what I want to be arguing for in these pages, I need to make it clear that I take seriously these Lutheran words of caution about acknowledging the "hiddenness" of God's present workings in history. But I don't want the caution to make us miss the occasions for joy that are also available to us. My intention in these pages, then, is to explore a way of viewing what is going on in the here and now with an eye toward the sorts of things in which God presently takes delight—and in which, then, we also should be taking delight.

The doctrine of common grace helps us, I am convinced, to put all of this into a proper theological perspective. And I am returning to that doctrine in these pages because I want to clear up what I see as some confusion about that doctrine, not only by those who oppose it but also by some who try to defend it. This necessitates looking at some neglected biblical themes about a God who continues to take delight in things that are happening in his creation.

3

The Divine Distance

Father Andrew Greeley was a sociologist with strong theological interests, and he also doubled as a best-selling novelist. His fiction contained frequent depictions of erotic sexuality—fairly mild stuff as graphic writing about sex goes these days, but still a little more than one might expect from a Catholic priest.

Father Greeley and I were speakers together on a university campus in the 1970s, and we had some good informal conversations. I found him a very reflective Christian thinker—we talked some about our common interest in C. S. Lewis's thought. We corresponded on and off after that, and I kept up on his (highly productive) scholarly writings.

I never discussed Calvinism with him, though. By the time I got around to reading his fine book *The Catholic Imagination*, published in 2000, which is where he offers his negative critique of the Calvinist perspective, Greeley had been seriously injured—never to recover—in a tragic accident. That book did inspire me to think about writing a similar one with the title *The Calvinist Imagination*. I doubt now that I will accomplish that—though perhaps some thoughts in this book will inspire a younger Reformed writer to do so.

A Failure of "Imagination"?

Those who have read Greeley's fiction will not be surprised to find that for him "the Catholic imagination" features a vibrant celebration of our lives as human creatures. The vitality of the Catholic engagement with reality stands, as he makes his case, in rather stark contrast to the Calvinist outlook.

Greeley sets up this contrast with an example from Lars von Trier's film *Breaking the Waves*. Bess is the film's heroine and she lives, Greeley tells us, in a "dour" Scottish Presbyterian community whose "Calvinist congregation [is] so suspicious of sacraments that it has removed bells from the bell tower of its church." When Bess experiences a "powerful pleasure in sexual love" with her husband, Greeley reports, "she thanks God, who seems, in a grudging Calvinist way, to approve of her passion."[1]

This failure to celebrate the erotic is for Greeley a symptom of a deeper malady. Calvinism lacks the kind of rich theology of the sacraments that for Catholicism is grounded in an even deeper sacramentalist view of reality. Not only are the bread and wine of the Eucharist the bearers of the divine reality but creation itself also embodies God's "real presence." And that is what Calvinism misses out on, he argues. The Calvinist perspective is a prime example of how Reformation theology fails to recognize this kind of divine "nearness" to created reality.

Greeley's theological hero in this regard is David Tracy— "theologian of the Enchanted Imagination"—to whom Greeley dedicates his book. Tracy makes it clear, says Greeley,

19

how Reformation theology has inhibited the artistic impulse. Here is how he summarizes Tracy's thought in his *Analogical Imagination*:

> Tracy noted that the classic works of Catholic theologians and artists tend to emphasize the presence of God in the world, while the classic works of Protestant theologians tend to emphasize the absence of God from the world. The Catholic writers stress the nearness of God to His creation, the Protestant writers the distance between God and His creation; the Protestants emphasize the risk of superstition and idolatry, the Catholics the dangers of a creation in which God is only marginally present.[2]

Actually, many of us in the neo-Calvinist movement have also voiced similar concerns about patterns that we see within our own Reformed ranks. We have critiqued, for example, a stark "body-soul dualism" that has promoted the very kind of ambivalence about sexual pleasure that Bess rebels against. And we have often wished for sacred spaces that provided at least a bit of what "the Catholic imagination" has to offer us by way of sacramentalist "mystery." While acknowledging that Greeley and Tracy overstate their case against Reformation thought and practice, we should admit that we can absorb some good things from what they have to say.

We also need to insist, of course, that Calvinists will rightly be more cautious than Greeley wants to be in assessing eroticism. Because we are so convinced of the all-pervasive character of human sinfulness, we Calvinists have made it one of our special spiritual assignments to keep reminding other Christians that there is no dimension of our created life that does not afford a real—and often deceptively subtle—opportunity for rebellion against the will of God. In particular, then, while we have no problem admitting that the erotic aspect of our lives was a part of the creation that God originally called good, we also want to point to the real danger that, under sinful conditions, the erotic can also become a staging area for a violation of the Creator's purposes. Our sexuality is one of the many aspects of fallen nature that needs to be redeemed.

Calvinism cannot compromise its insistence, then, on the pervasiveness of sin in our fallen condition. Another issue that emerges as we respond to the Greeley-Tracy type of divine "distance" challenge has to do with our basic understanding of God's ontological relationship to the creation.

Bridging the Gap

The Greeley-Tracy fondness for a doctrine of God's "nearness" to the creation makes my Calvinist antenna buzz a little. I learned early on that Reformed theology must preserve at all costs the unbridgeable ontological gap between Creator and creature. This was impressed upon me early on, when as a college student I read extensively the writings of Cornelius Van Til, who constantly referred to "the self-contained ontological Trinity."[3] God did not need to create anything in order to add to his own "being." God is the Wholly Other. A formula commonly attributed to Archbishop William Temple captures this nicely: "God minus the world equals God."

It is not a silly thing to worry about this when Catholics talk about divine nearness. The highly influential Jesuit theologian Karl Rahner seems to deny this unbridgeable gap in his discussion of the incarnation. We must not think of Christ, he says, "simply as someone who enters into our existence and its history from the outside, moves it a step further and also brings it to fulfillment in a certain sense, but then nevertheless leaves it behind." No, Rahner insists, the incarnation brought about a new kind of unity between humanity and God, wherein "God brings about man's self-transcendence into God," resulting in "an irrevocable kind of unity between this human reality and God."[4]

21

While it is unlikely that the Dutch Calvinist theologian Klaas Schilder ever read Rahner, he nicely characterized this kind of perspective when he warned against those who see Creator and creation as so "infatuated with each other" that it was inevitable that they would merge in an ontological sense.[5]

If Calvinism is to give a proper emphasis to a divine desire to be near the creation, it will have to be spelled out in terms of God's sovereign *decision* to draw near to that which he has created. God is not near to the creation in an ontological sense, but he *wills* to form a *relational* nearness. The triune God made a decision to create a world in which he, as the *totaliter aliter*, would take delight in all that he had made (Ps. 104:31). Human beings, in turn, were created to serve the Lord in obedience to his will, and the fall was the result of—in the traditional terminology of Reformed theology—an "ethical rebellion," a turning of the human will away from promoting the glory of God. But "God so loved the world" (John 3:16–17) that he chose to send the Son, the eternal Logos, into the world in order to restore a proper relationship between Creator and that which God had created.

For classical Reformed thought, the incarnation was essentially a rescue operation, a remedial project to restore God's original design for humanity in particular and the cosmos in general. And this means that, strictly speaking, the incarnation began with the birth of the Savior in Bethlehem and ended, in its earthly phase, with the ascension of Christ into the heavens. Thus the Heidelberg Catechism's explanation that Christ is not "according to his human nature . . . now . . . upon earth," for he has taken our flesh to heaven with him as the ascended Lord, and it is from there that he presently reigns over all things "according to his Godhead, majesty, grace, and Spirit."[6]

If we Reformed types are to celebrate God's "nearness" to us, then we have to make our case in terms of God's gracious "willings." God chose to create a world he would love. When fallenness came to permeate that creation, the Son came into the world, experiencing the full scope of our humanity, but without sin. Having accomplished his redemptive mission, he sends his Spirit into the world. Thus, we are gifted with the nearness of creational love, with incarnational identification, and with the presence of the Spirit.

Learning from Heretics

I have mused in print on occasion about having "favorite heretics"—people who are wrong about important matters, but in their very wrongness they prod us to clarify certain of our own cherished beliefs.[7] Some of my own favorites are thinkers and movements that challenge me as a Calvinist to be aware of the possible dangers that come with a strong affirmation of the ontological gap between Creator and creation.

I have been particularly fascinated in this regard by three persons whose ideas in early nineteenth-century America inspired "ontological nearness" movements: Joseph Smith, Mary Baker Eddy, and Ralph Waldo Emerson. They represented quite different metaphysical perspectives, of course, with Smith espousing a divine corporeality, Eddy advocating an "everything is mind" perspective, and Emerson preaching the need to evolve "spiritually" beyond our present self-imposed limits.

What I find significant, though, is that each of them was reacting against a religious environment shaped by the Calvinism associated with New England Puritanism. And certain strands of Puritan thought, while rightly emphasizing the metaphysical distance between Creator and creation, often fostered a sense of a parallel unbridgeable *spiritual* gap between God and his human creatures. It should not surprise us, then, that movements such as Mormonism, Christian Science, and transcendentalism emerged in that environment out of a desire to bring the divine nearer to the likes of us—to reduce the distance between God and human beings—even if we must deeply regret that they did so by also shrinking the distance of Being rather than by drawing on corrective teachings that can be found within orthodox Christian theology.

I have been helped in thinking about this by Janice Knight and her 1994 book *Orthodoxies in Massachusetts*. Knight, an English professor at the University of Chicago, distinguishes between two schools of thought within the orthodox Calvinism of American Puritanism. One view, represented by William Ames, depicts God as a distant sovereign before whom human beings must live in reverence in the presence of transcendent mystery. In this conception, a pattern of spirituality developed where the believer's relationship to God was dominated by metaphors like master/servant and king/subject. To be sure, a "warmer" piety often showed up in this context, but always against the background that everything else had to be understood with reference to God as "an exacting lord" and a "demanding covenanter."[8]

Knight finds a significant alternative within Puritanism to Ames's conception of sovereign power as the primary attribute of God. She details the ways in which some American Puritans looked to Richard Sibbes, Ames's contemporary in Old England, for their theological inspiration. The Sibbesians offered a Calvinist conception of God in whom mercy and not power was primary. Here was a clear alternative to the Amesian view of a deity for whom, as Knight puts it, "the only bridge was the contractual covenant, not the personal Christ."[9]

Sibbesian Calvinism never abandoned the deep conviction of divine sovereignty. What it did, however, was downplay any notion of an *arbitrary* sovereignty by stressing images of divine intimacy. It is interesting that Sibbes explicitly addresses the divine distance issue in setting forth his views on the possibilities of intimacy with the divine. Believers can be assured, he writes, that God "applies himself to us, and hath taken upon himself near relations, that he might be near us in goodness. He is a father, and everywhere to maintain us. He is a husband, and everywhere to help. He is a friend, and everywhere to comfort and counsel. So his love it is a near love. Therefore he has taken upon him the nearest relations, that we may never want [i.e., miss out on] God and the testimonies of his love."[10]

In making his case here, Sibbes employs images relating to the First Person of the Trinity. And effectively so. There is also much to be gained, though, from looking at the ways in which the other two divine persons reinforce and expand our theological grasp of that spiritual nearness.

I see the theological explorations of Abraham Kuyper and Herman Bavinck as pointing the way to a more robust trinitarian theology of God's nearness to the creation than we often find in the Reformed theological tradition. Fundamental to properly appreciating these pointers is the need to begin where the Bible begins—with a scenario in which God takes delight in the rich complexity of the creation that he calls into being by his sovereign will.

4

"That's Good!"

Not long before he died, my friend Lewis Smedes completed his memoir about his spiritual journey. Smedes was always an engaging writer, and he was at his best in this little book. Here is one of my favorite passages, in which he talks about his first day in a literature class at Calvin College, having just transferred to the Grand Rapids school from the Moody Bible Institute.

[The professor] introduced me that day to a God the likes of whom I had never even heard about—a God who liked elegant sentences and was offended by dangling modifiers. Once you believe this, where can you stop? If the Maker of the Universe admired words well put together, think of how he must love sound thought well put together, and if he loved sound think-ing, how he must love a Bach concerto; and if he loved a Bach concerto, think of how he prized any human effort to bring a foretaste, be it ever so small, of his Kingdom of justice and peace and happiness to the victimized people of the world. In short, I met the Maker of the Universe, who loved the world he made and was dedicated to its redemption. I found the joy of the Lord, not at a prayer meeting, but in English Composition 101.[1]

Smedes was a neo-Calvinist—he had a large poster hanging on his office wall of a famous Dutch political cartoon of Abraham Kuyper's face. And in this passage, Smedes is capturing in graphic terms the basic point of Kuyper's oft-quoted manifesto: "There is not one square inch of the entire creation about which Jesus Christ does not cry out, 'This is mine! This belongs to me!'"[2]

I have quoted that manifesto hundreds of times in lectures and writings. It is a powerful affirmation of the authority of Jesus Christ over all created reality. And I have found it to be a highly effective way to introduce people to the basics of Kuyper's thought.

All by itself, however, Kuyper's proclamation can be used to reinforce some worrisome patterns. An obvious one is triumphalism. Christ owns all of this territory, which means that unbelievers are occupying turf that does not belong to them—so let's go out and take those square inches back in the name of Christ!

Or someone could take the "mine!" of Kuyper's manifesto as suggesting a divine petulance, like the child who is upset when someone else has his toy: "That's mine! You can't have it!"

What Smedes's examples point us to, however, is a spirit of divine affection. God *loves* well-written poems, Bach concertos, and sound arguments. They are things in which the Lord takes pride and pleasure because they are manifestations of his creating purposes for the world he still loves.

I was once invited to take the stage after a performance at a theater, to discuss the production with the person who wrote the play. He began our conversation by thanking everyone who had been a part of the production that evening: the stage crew, the director, the actors. "It is simply thrilling," he said, "to see the play of mine come to life in this marvelous way!" That captures the kind of thing that Kuyper had in mind in giving us a picture of Christ crying out "mine!"

Created "Swarms"

This love of God for the whole creation is stated clearly in John 3:17. The previous verse, of course, is the marvelous declaration—arguably the most quoted from the Bible on the subject—of God's love for sinners. The beautiful message of individual salvation is here framed by the divine love for "the world," which in the Greek is *kosmos*, the larger created order. And Jesus goes on to affirm, in verse 17, that this redemptive love is also cosmic in character, for the Son was not sent "into the world [*kosmos*] to condemn the world [*kosmos*], but to save the world [*kosmos*] through him" (NIV).

I will put it bluntly: salvation is not just about restoring individual sinners to a right relationship with God—although it certainly includes that. Redemption is cosmic in scope.

God's love for the nonhuman creation is evident in Psalm 104, a hymn to God's creating power and goodness, where there is almost no reference to human beings at all. The psalmist speaks of God stretching "out the heavens like a tent" (v. 2) and creating winds, fires, and the foundations of the earth. And he goes into considerable detail about springs of water, wild animals, birds, grass, wine, oil, bread, trees, storms, goats, coneys—and much more. And then two key confessions from the psalmist: "O Lord, how manifold are your works!" (v. 24) and "May the Lord rejoice in his works" (v. 31).

This hymn of praise clearly echoes the creation account in Genesis, where there is actually quite a bit that happens between God and created reality before we human beings enter the scene.

I don't remember ever hearing a sermon on Genesis 1 that inspired me—or even one that was *meant* to inspire me but failed to do so. In my growing-up years I heard sermons in which we were encouraged to understand the creation story literally. And over the decades I have heard lectures about "the days of creation" and witnessed debates—not a few of them angry exchanges—about how the world came into being and about the origins of human life. But no sermons on the first chapter of the Bible that simply edified my soul.

And yet Genesis 1 is a marvelously edifying chapter. Without getting into the interpretation of "day" here, the creation account is a wonderful narrative about how God spent five days taking delight in his creation, even before human beings came on the scene.

On the first day, God calls light into being, and then he pronounces, "That's good!" Then the separation of the sea from the dry land, and once again, "That's good!" Then vegetation: "That's good!" Sun and moon: "That's good!"

I especially like the "living creatures" day. The English Standard Version has the Lord saying, "Let the waters swarm with swarms of living creatures" (Gen. 1:20). I picture here God looking down on an empty pond, and as a result of his sovereign command the pond is suddenly swarming with tadpoles and minnows and turtles and bugs skimming across the surface. And the Lord looks down on that swarmy pond and exclaims in delight, "That's really good!"

Five days of that kind of divine rejoicing in the nonhuman content of the creation! And then, when the Lord creates the man and the woman he tells them to take good care of all that he has been producing over the previous five days.

"Do It Again!"

G. K. Chesterton has a nice way of capturing the nature of God's appreciation for the nonhuman creation. The Lord, says

Chesterton, has a way of taking delight in things that is more like that of a child than of an adult.

> Because children have abounding vitality, because they are in spirit fierce and free, therefore they want things repeated and unchanged. They always say, "Do it again"; and the grown-up person does it again until he is nearly dead. For grown-up people are not strong enough to exult in monotony. But perhaps God is strong enough to exult in monotony. It is possible that God says every morning, "Do it again" to the sun; and every evening, "Do it again" to the moon. It may not be automatic necessity that makes all daisies alike; it may be that God makes every daisy separately, but has never got tired of making them.[3]

Well, whether Chesterton has it exactly right about the divine production of daisies, he certainly is capturing something important about God's delight in the nonhuman creation, as is evident in the Genesis account as well as in Psalm 104. Again, when it comes to things that please the Lord, it is not all about us. God is glorified also by plants and animals and rivers and mountains. It is not insignificant that after the wonderful song to the Lamb in Revelation 5, where the heavenly courts rejoice over the salvation of people from every tribe and tongue and nation (Rev. 5:9–10), the Seer reports yet another hymn, this one sung by the likes of panda bears and gophers and hawks and sea bass:

> Then I heard every creature in heaven and on earth and under the earth and on the sea, and all that is in them, saying:
>
> > "To him who sits on the throne and to the Lamb
> > be praise and honor and glory and power,
> > for ever and ever!" (Rev. 5:13 NIV)

Why make something of this—the fact that God delights in, and is glorified by, the nonhuman creation? For one thing—and this is a bit of an aside—to recognize this has profound implications for present-day environmental concerns. As already mentioned, when human beings do arrive on the scene in Genesis 1, the Creator tells them to "have dominion" over that which the Lord has already put in place. I do not think it is stretching the Genesis narrative to understand that mandate in this way: God has been enjoying what he has already created—the planets, mountains, birds, fish—and when he fashions human beings in his own image he wants to be clear about the fact that he wants human beings to take care of that nonhuman creation, with an awareness that God is very fond of what he is placing under human management.

But the main point is this: the Creator of the world has very broad interests. The Lord rejoices in all of his works. God is really fond of daisies and deer and oak trees. This means, then, that we have to take this broader divine agenda seriously. God's creating and redeeming work certainly focuses in a very special way on human beings. The Lord is glorified by our obedient service. The triune God desires our worship—so much so that God was so intent upon demonstrating his love for us that "while we still were sinners Christ died for us" (Rom. 5:8 NRSV). But it isn't *all* about us, as individual human beings who have been redeemed through the blood of the cross. As important as we are in God's renewing purposes, we fit into a much larger divine agenda.

To put it a little differently: God has multiple purposes in the divine plan for both creation and redemption. This has not always been emphasized in the Reformed tradition. Often our focus has been on God's seeking his own glory—with the accounts of what it means for God to be glorified focusing exclusively on his having the elect direct their obedience and praise to him.

Neo-Calvinism has worked consistently to lay out a larger scenario, in which God intended from the very beginning that human obedience to his creating purposes would consist not merely in having individuals glorify him by their personal

31

worship. They were to bring him glory by filling the earth with the processes and products of human cultural formation. These are things in which God takes delight—and when God's human creatures also take delight in them they are genuinely honoring the Creator's purposes. Even when the curse of human fallenness pervaded the creation, God did not give up on these original designs. The patterns of a renewed cultural obedience were made possible by Christ's atoning work. Furthermore, under the conditions of fallenness the Lord takes delight even when his original purposes shine through beyond the scope of the elect community—when, for example, an unbeliever produces a well-crafted poem, or when a film sets forth a narrative of human flourishing, or when signs of justice are seen in public policies implemented in the larger society.

The final results of the divine love of "many-ness" are depicted nicely in Herman Bavinck's end-time scenario:

> The state of glory, Scripture tells us, will be rich and splendid beyond all description. We look for a new heaven, a new earth, a new humanity, a restored universe, an ever-progressing development never again disturbed by sin. To that end, the creation and the fall, Adam and Christ, nature and grace, faith and unbelief, election and reprobation—all work together, each in its own way, not only consequently but in concert. Indeed, even the present world, along with its history, is as such already an ongoing revelation of God's perfections. It will continue to exert its influence in depth and in breadth also in the coming dispensation, and to furnish a new humanity with ever new reasons for the worship and glorification of God.[4]

This "many-ness" scope of God's continuing embrace of his creation comes to a new stage of fulfillment—one with cosmic effects—as a result of the death and resurrection of Jesus Christ. We can now proclaim boldly, the apostle Paul tells us, that Jesus "is before all things, and in him all things hold together" (Col. 1:17). And against the background of that reality, Paul can recognize the rule of Christ over all dimensions of our lives: "Whatever you do, whether in word or deed, do it all in the name of the Lord Jesus, giving thanks to God the Father through him" (3:17 NIV).

Most serious Christians these days would accept the idea that our work matters to God—even that God takes delight when a believer accomplishes some task well or produces something that conforms to God's creating and renewing designs. Most Reformed Christians, given our insistence on important patterns of continuity between the Older and Newer Covenants, would also insist on a connection between assignments issued by God to ancient Israel and to the New Testament people of God in areas of economic life, care for the earth, norms for political justice, and the like.

But when confronting the question of the accomplishments in these areas on the part of unbelievers, disagreements quickly emerge. God may take delight in a painting composed by a Christian artist, but what about one painted by Pablo Picasso? Or how does God view a lovingly faithful fifty-year marriage between two atheists?

The doctrine of common grace has been central to Calvinism's—and particularly to neo-Calvinism's—efforts to account for an attitude of divine favor toward many of the products and processes of cultural engagement beyond the boundaries of the company of the redeemed. But that doctrine has by no means been universally accepted within the Reformed community. Indeed, it has on occasion been the cause of deep divisions.

And even where there has been formal agreement among Calvinists that the doctrine is important to acknowledge, quite different understandings of what the teaching amounts to are at work. My own understanding is clearly on the positive— even expansive—side of the spectrum, as will be obvious as I develop my case here.

5

Assessing the Natural Mind

When I reflected recently in some published autobiographical thoughts about the beginnings of my own theological pilgrimage,[1] I reported that the first serious theological piece of writing I had ever read was Cornelius Van Til's ninety-five-page booklet *Common Grace*. What Van Til discussed in those pages was all new to me. I was in my late teens at the time, and I had recently become an ardent Calvinist through the combined influence of reading wonderful sermons by Charles Spurgeon—particularly the one titled "Election"—and being led through a careful study of the Canons of Dort by J. B. Hulst, who was a Christian Reformed pastor in Orange City, Iowa, where I spent my first two college years.

The Iowa college that I attended, Northwestern, was a two-year school at the time, so I transferred to Houghton College to finish my undergraduate studies. Back home in New Jersey during the summer before entering Houghton, I spent much time talking about Calvinism with John Richard DeWitt, a pastor in Paterson who was later to join the faculty at Reformed Theological Seminary. De Witt was convinced that I needed to go deeper into Calvinist thought—especially since I was soon to study at Houghton College, a Wesleyan school—so he urged me to read Van Til's short book during that summer.

Van Til's Influence

I found reading Van Til exciting. I actually read the booklet several times, trying hard to understand what were for me new theological ideas couched in technical theological vocabulary. On the very first page Van Til referred to Abraham Kuyper, Klaas Schilder, and Herman Hoeksema—names previously unknown to me. In an important sense, that first page, with those names, set a theological agenda for me that I would pursue to the present.

As I look back at my experience, almost six decades ago, of reading that short but theologically compact book as a nineteen-year-old, I try to grasp just what it was that excited me so much. The excitement certainly had to do with the way Van Til's discussion showed me that Calvinism had a much broader scope than simply addressing issues about individual salvation. But the idea of a *common* grace also spoke to my growing enthusiasm for engaging ideas that came to me from studying non-Christian writers. I could wrestle with the writings of, for example, an Emerson and a Hemingway (I was an English major) with the assurance that I was not being disobedient to God when exploring intellectual matters beyond the scope of the Christian community.

It took me several years to realize, however, that there was some irony in the idea of being inspired by Van Til to engage non-Christian thinkers in an appreciative manner. Reading his little book had introduced me to the *idea* of a common

35

grace, which in turn made me open to learning from thinkers beyond the scope of the Christian community. But the actual substance of what Van Til meant by common grace did not leave much room for a genuinely *appreciative* engagement with non-Christian thought.

For Van Til, God has a "favorable attitude toward all" in the sense that all human beings share in the "early common perfect nature" of Adam in his unfallen state. In the original unity of humankind in Adam, all humans were, in the sight of God, "mandate-hearers and covenant-keepers." In the beginning, then, God could look with unmixed delight at the human race as represented in the unfallen Adam: "God beheld all the works of His hands, and behold they were very good. God was pleased with them."[2]

Post-fall, though, we no longer have a common humanity. The elect are moving toward glorification, while the reprobates are heading for destruction. When the process of history is completed, the radical difference between the two classes of human beings will be fully evident. In the here and now, however, the process of historical differentiation is taking place. While in reality they represent two different manifestations of humanity—elect and reprobate—the non-elect are not yet fully "epistemologically self-conscious."[3] While they no longer possess that which they had in their shared created-but-unfallen humanness in Adam, neither have they yet arrived at the fully actualized reprobate state of consciousness that is their destiny. Because of this we can say in the present that "there is a certain attitude of favor of God toward a generality of mankind, and a certain good before God in the life of the historically undeveloped unbeliever." As the process of historical differentiation continues, however, "it becomes increasingly difficult to observe that which is common," since in our actual history "God increases His attitude of wrath upon the reprobate as time goes on, until at the end of time, at the great consummation of history, their condition has caught up with their state."[4]

In this little book, Van Til criticizes both Kuyper and Bavinck for their failure to develop their understanding of common grace in a manner consistent with their Calvinist principles. He does commend them for how they "led the way in modern times in the direction of working out a truly Protestant theology. But they have not quite had the courage to go consistently along the path they have marked out for us."[5]

In pointing to the "vagueness inherent" in the way the two of them treat common grace,[6] Van Til makes his case on several fronts. At times he accuses them of being too mired in "scholasticism," with the result that they have not broken sufficiently with the Catholic conception of natural theology. At other points he even sees them as much too influenced by thoughts associated with Plato and Immanuel Kant. But the underlying issue in all of this for Van Til is that the two neo-Calvinist pioneers fail to be consistent in holding to the doctrine of total depravity. While they boldly proclaim the reality of the antithesis between a consistent biblical worldview and other perspectives, they do not follow through adequately on their affirmations. In the final analysis they give too much credit to the noetic abilities of the unredeemed human mind. They fail to abide, Van Til says, by the biblical depiction of the "would-be autonomous man" as someone who is "dead in trespasses and sins [and] lives in the valley of the blind, while yet he insists that he alone dwells in the light."[7]

A Personal Looking-Back

It is difficult to figure out, in light of this depiction of the unredeemed consciousness, why a Christian should actually appreciate—take delight in—a Picasso painting or an Emerson essay. To the degree that God is favorable toward non-elect individuals, for Van Til it is because God looks back to the pre-fallen state and sees them included in the generic humanness that God invested in Adam as the federal head of the human race. But post-fall "God no longer in any sense *classifies* them in a generality with the elect. It was only at an earlier date, before the consummation of their wicked striving was made complete, that God *even in a sense* classified them with the elect."[8] There may still be, Van Til says, some things in the lives of the non-elect that strike us as admirable. But those things are because the non-elect have not yet become fully self-conscious of the direction they have taken in their rebellion against the Creator. When we see admirable traits and achievements in the unredeemed, then, we should judge them to be only "relatively good" phenomena in what is in fact the "absolutely evil" character of depraved humanity.[9]

It is difficult to see any of this as providing us with genuine encouragement for pursuing a life of positive engagement with the works of culture produced beyond the boundaries of the Christian community. And yet that is precisely the kind of encouragement I have claimed to receive from reading Van Til's *Common Grace* in my late teens. Was I simply confused at the time about what I was reading?

Well, while there was certainly some degree of failure on my part to comprehend the implications of what I was reading, I did get some things right. Van Til's strong emphasis on the depravity of the sinful mind led him to insist that we not take at face value apparent agreements with what non-Christians are setting forth. The non-elect are in a state of rebellion against their Creator, but they are not yet fully aware of the implications of that rebellion. Believers and unbelievers see reality in radically different ways. We do not, Van Til insists, share the same "facts." The antithesis between our two ways of experiencing reality even shows up, he argues, on the basic level of how each class of human beings "weighs and measures."[10] But the awareness of this difference is not yet fully realized. At this present stage of history, says Van Til, "unbelievers are more self-conscious epistemologically in the dimension of religion than [they are] in the dimension of mathematics. The process of differentiation has not proceeded as far in the lower, as it has in the higher, dimensions."[11]

That is still not very encouraging. But my teenage self was not completely clueless. What I rightly took away from reading Van Til was that since we Christians should not presuppose large areas of "neutral" thought shared with unbelievers, it is important to approach the Christian intellectual life with a desire to develop our own epistemological self-consciousness. I learned from him about the need to think deeply and carefully about the issues, promoting clarity about how Christian presuppositions shape a uniquely biblically based perspective on all areas of human concern. I learned from Van Til that critical engagement with non-Christian thought is a *necessity* within the believing community. And that conviction has stayed with me, even though it has come to be expressed in a different way than Van Til intended. I have always taken seriously his insistence on being self-consciously Christian in engaging with non-Christian thought. Reading him served me well by introducing me to a profoundly important theological discussion—even though, as I will be explaining, I soon found myself enjoying non-Christian contributions more than his theology of common grace allowed.

6

Is "Restraint" Enough?

I had the same type of experience as Lew Smedes when I encountered the Lord in an English class during my junior year at Houghton College. As an English major, one of the first advanced courses I took was in nineteenth-century British nonfiction literature taught by a legendary Houghton professor, Dr. Josephine Rickard—"Doc Jo," we all called her. One of the writers whom she assigned was Thomas Carlyle, a brilliant Scottish thinker who had abandoned the convictions of his Christian upbringing and was good at directing his satirical skills at some key aspects of the Christian faith. I found his writings intriguing—which was for me a bit of a guilty pleasure. I enjoyed reading him, and on the day when we were to discuss Carlyle's writings, I went to class wondering what Doc Jo—a deeply spiritual Wesleyan who was known to spend her early morning hours praying for missionaries—would say about Carlyle.

As was her practice, Doc Jo began our seminar that day by asking us to bow our heads in prayer. We did, and there was a bit of a pause, so I looked up to see what was happening. Doc Jo's eyes were closed and her face was lifted upward, breaking out with what I can only describe as a heavenly glow. And then she began to pray by thanking the Lord for Thomas Carlyle—for his many God-given talents, including his wonderful way of putting words together.

Thus my Smedesian moment. The Lord loved good writing. I did not have to feel guilty about reading people who were not Christians, and I could actually take delight in what they wrote.

Considering Specific Cases

In my recent rereading of Cornelius Van Til's writings on common grace, I find little to go on for figuring out what he would say about a well-written passage authored by a Thomas Carlyle. Would Van Til tell me that my strong inclination to take delight in reading such a passage is simply based on theological confusion? Or is it permissible to see an element of the "relatively good" in his writing, as long as I am clear about the "absolute evil" of the state of consciousness toward which he is moving? Instead of giving me any specific guidance on these matters, Van Til wanted to issue a general warning about the dangers of positing a "neutral" turf that the elect occupy with the non-elect. To start setting up standards or beliefs that allow us to assume common ground with unbelievers is, Van Til insisted, to fall into the same trap that Scholastics in the Catholic tradition have set for themselves. "Any area of commonness, that is, any area of commonness without qualification however small, is a justification for larger areas of commonness, till at last there is but one common area." We must choose between the way of "the would-be autonomous man" or that of "the believer, knowing himself to be a creature of God."[1]

I don't find much help in that on how to decide whether I can take delight in the writings of a Thomas Carlyle. It is possible, of course, that Van Til meant to allow for some kind of appreciation for things produced by non-Christians under the category of the "relatively good." But his warnings not to allow for any "common ground" with unbelievers do not encourage us to risk taking too much delight in what they produce.

Daniel Strange, who draws directly on Van Til's theology for his own scholarly efforts, is more helpful than Van Til is in making extensive use of the Van Tilian framework for assessing the beliefs and practices of unbelievers. In his recent book on the theology of religions, Strange directly addresses the reality that non-Christians do often seem to be in line with Christian goals and values in what they aspire to achieve. "How are we theologically to explain these things," he asks, "while still upholding the principle of the antithesis" between two radically differing ways of experiencing reality? Does this mean that there can be in our relationship with unbelievers some "elements of continuity" within the larger pattern of our differences? Strange, following Van Til, thinks not. But he does elaborate on this assessment. The apparent continuity, he says, is due to "the non-salvific work of the Holy Spirit who, in his common grace, restrains sin and excites to a civic righteousness." This divine operation functions in spite of the depraved state of those whom it touches. "Non-Christians," says Strange, "live off 'borrowed capital' or, better, steal the 'fruit' of the Christian worldview and claim it for their own."[2]

There are two key concepts in these remarks by Strange that deserve some attention in thinking about the apparent goodness that shows up in the lives of unbelievers: first, there is the *theft* imagery, which depicts unbelievers as stealing that which properly belongs to the Christian worldview. Then there is the reference to common grace's role in *restraining* the sinfulness of depraved humanity. Each of them deserves our attention.

"Unlawful Possession"

Saint Augustine had no problem with the notion of Christians taking ideas from non-Christians and making them our own. In doing so, he argues, we often are merely repossessing that which rightly belongs to us. He draws a parallel on this to what the people of Israel did when they departed from Egypt. They took with them some of the "vessels and ornaments of gold and silver, and garments," which they "appropriated to themselves, designing them for a better use, [and] not doing this on their own authority, but by the command of God."[3]

That same kind of appropriation applies, he says, to matters of the mind. He asks us to consider the accomplishments of the Greek philosophers, particularly Plato and his followers, who have developed a system of thought that Augustine sees as containing much that is "true and in harmony with our faith." We don't have to feel bad about putting these ideas to our own use, he says, because in doing so we are simply reclaiming them "from those who have unlawful possession of it." Those ideas contain "gold and silver, which they did not create themselves, but dug out of the mines of God's providence which are everywhere scattered abroad." When we Christians recognize the need to depart "in spirit from the miserable fellowship of these men," we have every right to take these ideas with us, putting them now "to a Christian use."[4]

So how does that help me in understanding the good things that I enjoyed as a college student in the writings of Thomas Carlyle? He certainly was indebted in his thinking to his Christian past. His Calvinist upbringing obviously had a formative influence on his intellectual development. So does that mean that we should think of ourselves as having the right as Christians to take back from Carlyle that which in his writing was "borrowed capital" from a Christian worldview?

That seems to me to be too easy. One obvious factor that it does not account for is Carlyle's unique literary creativity. Here, for example, is the opening paragraph of his great *Sartor Resartus*—a title that translates as "a tailor re-tailored" or, as some have suggested in order to capture Carlyle's satirical intent, "the patcher re-patched":

> Considering our present advanced state of culture, and how the Torch of Science has now been brandished and borne about, with more or less effect, for five thousand years and upwards; how, in these times especially, not only the Torch still burns, and perhaps more fiercely than ever, but innumerable Rushlights, and Sulphur-matches, kindled thereat, are also glancing in every direction, so that not the smallest cranny or dog-hole in Nature or Art can remain unilluminated,—it might strike the reflective mind with some surprise that hitherto little or nothing of a fundamental character, whether in the way of Philosophy or History, has been written on the subject of Clothes.[5]

I still find that opening paragraph of *Sartor Resartus* as delightful as I did when I first read it as a nineteen-year-old. And now, as then, I feel no need to reclaim those sentences from Carlyle. Yes, he was in a state of unbelief when he wrote them, but knowing that does not make me see these sentences as his "unlawful possession." I don't want to "seize" them from him. I want him to "keep" them. They are an expression of *his* gifts. So, like Doc Jo, I thank the Lord for Thomas Carlyle himself.

All of that is to explain with reference to a concrete case why I find the neo-Calvinist perspective to be so helpful. It does not require me to see unbelievers simply as "channeling" words and thoughts that come from God. In producing admirable cultural achievements, they are being themselves. We are right in expressing appreciation for their talents.

The Scope of Divine "Restraint"

In stipulating that, in the workings of common grace, God "re-strains sin and excites to a civic righteousness," Daniel Strange is following Van Til in endorsing the formulations of the doctrine of common grace set forth by the Christian Reformed Church's synod, meeting in Kalamazoo, Michigan, in 1924. That synod's affirmations on the subject led to the departure of Herman Hoeksema and his followers from the Christian Reformed denomination and also set the agenda for much of the controversy over common grace in North American Calvinism during the twentieth century.[6]

That 1924 synodical gathering saw itself as drawing directly on Abraham Kuyper's theology in adopting its "Three Points" on the subject. There is, the synod declared, a non-salvific disposition of divine favor toward all human beings that manifests itself in these three ways: (1) the bestowal of natural gifts, such as rain and sunshine, upon creatures in general; (2) the restraining of sin in human affairs, so that the unredeemed do not produce all the evil that their depraved natures might otherwise bring about; and (3) the ability of unbelievers to perform acts of civic good.[7]

In these debates, the Hoeksema party insisted that none of the realities covered by these three factors require the acknowledgment of a posture of divine favor toward the non-elect. A robust doctrine of divine providence, they argued, with a particular focus on the providential "restraint" of sin, can do all the necessary theological work. And I think they make a plausible case in this regard—at least if we restrict our attention only to the first two points.

On the first point, for example, Hoeksema saw no reason to take the Matthew 5:45 passage as affirming divine favor toward the non-elect in bestowing natural gifts that benefit believer and unbeliever alike. In the lives of the non-elect, such things as "rain, fruitful seasons, and food and gladness" serve the depraved practices of those who are outside of Christ. They are put to use in the "ways of iniquity and destruction" by persons who are "objects of His wrath and damnation."[8] While I certainly am not inclined to follow Hoeksema on this, I cannot think of an argument that would convince him that he has it wrong.

The second point certainly expresses something about divine providence that any Calvinist would take to be a matter of basic theology: through providential means, God restrains the power of sin in the world. Depraved sinners do not do all the evil they are capable of doing. A common image here among Calvinists is that of a leash on a rabid dog. Without the leash the dog would cause much harm, but the leash restricts his ability to do so. The leash does not "tame" the dog or cure the rabies. It just holds him back.

Again, not much to argue about there. The question, of course, is whether that explains *all* the apparent good we think we see happening beyond the boundaries of the believing community. And this is the important issue that emerges in relation to the third point: "the ability of unbelievers to perform acts of civic good." Is this simply another manifestation of providential "restraint," understood as God using the leash to hold evil back? Or do we need to posit an "internal" capacity to do good in the life of the unbeliever?

Hoeksema is adamant in his refusal to allow anything "internal" in this regard. Allowing for such is in reality, he says, "a denial of the total depravity of man. For, when we set aside all sophistical reasonings and hopeless attempts to show how a totally depraved man is able to do good works and a wholly corrupt tree may still bring forth good fruit, the bare fact remains that by this theory [of common grace] man, as he actually reveals himself in this world, is not totally depraved and wholly corrupt." Thus, for Hoeksema, in common-grace theology the radical antithesis between belief and unbelief is "obliterated and the chasm between the church and the world is removed. . . . It is only by a good deal of sophistry that this real implication of the third point can be denied."[9]

I already revealed my hand on this matter in confessing that I find writers like Thomas Carlyle producing genuinely good things in which God wants us to take delight. In order to make the case for seeing things that way, we can turn to Kuyper and Bavinck for help. But this also requires getting clear about what is at stake for our Calvinist commitments in pushing in the direction of their kind of expansive theology of culture.

7

A Pause for Some "Meta-Calvinist" Considerations

This is a point where a Calvinist has to make a decision. And the decision is a very basic one. It has a "meta" character to it. It is a decision about how we are going to hold on to our basic Calvinist convictions. In making this decision it is important to take Herman Hoeksema seriously in his challenge to those of us who want to proceed in offering a case for taking delight in non-Christian thought and action: Are we really serious about the doctrine of total depravity?

In an important sense, of course, there can be only one answer on this for a Calvinist. The doctrine of total depravity is nonnegotiable. Hold to it we must. But there is still a decision to be made about *how* we are to hold to this doctrine. How should we integrate our belief in shared depravity with other things that we believe and experience?

But it isn't only the defender of common grace who must make a decision here. Those who deny common grace also have to make a decision at this point. And it is important to understand why.

Divine Empathy?

David Engelsma is a firm opponent of common grace. He has been a leading theologian in the Hoeksema tradition. He is also a friend. We have debated with each other about our deep differences, but always with charity—indeed, with an eagerness on each of our parts to clarify our positions in response to each other.

In a short (one-hundred-page) book that he wrote in response to my defense of common grace, he sets forth his sharp disagreement with the idea that God has a favorable attitude toward some things done by non-Christians. Engelsma does not hesitate to put his case with bluntness: "All the works of unbelievers," he says, "are foul with depravity of seeking man rather than God. Upon these works falls the wrath of God, now and in the final judgment."[1]

Engelsma discusses in some detail my insistence that God shows "empathy" with some of the joys and sorrows of the non-elect. He specifically considers two examples that I cite in my book *He Shines in All That's Fair* to make my point about divine empathy.[2] One is a shocking news report I had heard during the war in Bosnia Herzegovina, about a Muslim woman who was gang-raped by "Christian" soldiers. When they violated that woman, they also killed her infant child. God, I said, grieved with the young mother in her despair.

My second example was a hypothetical case of a Christian therapist who helped a couple on the brink of divorce—with no sign of religious faith in their lives—to ask each other for forgiveness and to reconcile. In that moment of reconciliation, I asked, did the Lord not take pleasure in what had happened?

While Engelsma acknowledges that there is something "powerful" about such considerations, he insists that the power is due to the fact that this sort of situation is not "thought through with carefully reasoned propositions. It is simply *felt*."[3] And as a result, "our own feelings especially of sympathy with the suffering, and our natural impulse to improve the world, regardless that we must cooperate with those who deny Christ, have a way of setting aside the confessions and blinding us to the testimony of Scripture."[4]

My Protestant Reformed friend does go on, though, to concede that on one level our Christian feelings of empathy toward non-Christians can be legitimate. "The Christian is related to other humans by the strong ties of mutual flesh and blood. Out of this shared humanity wells up empathy." In honoring these human ties, then, we are acting in accordance with God's will for our lives. God does want us to love those with whom we share the bond of humanness. We are to love our neighbors. But *God himself* is not bound by that obligation to love. "God's relation to these same humans, however, is not that of neighbor." As reprobates, they are objects of God's wrath. They are, Engelsma remarks, "guilty, foul creatures," and the Lord "curses all that's foul."[5] Thus God commands us to have neighborly feelings toward persons whom he hates.

Choosing for Common Grace

The defender of common grace, says Engelsma, having abandoned an undiluted understanding of total depravity, "confuses providence with grace." Even John Calvin, he says, commits this error on occasion, failing to be clear about the fact that "the abilities of the heathen in the arts and sciences, as also the regard for virtue by certain of the 'noble pagans,' which Calvin sometimes attributed to a grace of God in them, are the effects of providence."[6]

The "sometimes" in that comment about Calvin is important. While the Reformer strongly believed that God restrains sinful individuals from doing all the evil they are capable of, he did not understand God's good purposes in the world solely in terms of the providential restraint of sin.

Calvin never lost the appreciation he had cultivated in his legal studies for several Greek and Roman writers, especially Seneca. In his *Institutes*, Calvin points his readers to an "admirable light of truth shining" in the thoughts of pagan thinkers—evidence, he says, that "the mind of man, though fallen and perverted from its wholeness," can still be "clothed and ornamented with God's excellent gifts." To refuse to accept the truth produced by such minds, then, is "to dishonor the Spirit of God,"[7] who imparts to such persons a "peculiar grace."[8]

Calvin had made a choice. He decided to trust his experience of delight in reading pagan writers and to make room in his theology for a positive evaluation of their accomplishments. And the choice was for him a profoundly spiritual and theological one. It was a choice to honor the work of the Holy Spirit beyond the boundaries of the Christian community.

Engelsma makes a different choice. He encounters those same writings by ancient authors and pronounces that there is nothing but corruption in what they wrote. Cicero, Plato, Aristotle—we must count them all as "guilty, foul creatures" whose writings are not acceptable to the Lord, who "curses all that's foul."[9]

Abraham Kuyper is very explicit about his conviction that, in making the choice for common grace, he is not denying the doctrine of total depravity. In the light of the good things that we see in the lives of unbelievers, he argues, "either [we] surrender our confession of the deadly character of sin, or [we] hold on to that confession with all our might, but then also confess along with it that there is a common grace at work that in many cases restrains the full, deadly effect of sin."[10]

Kuyper addresses the issue directly with reference to the Heidelberg Catechism's verdict that our human depravity means that "we are wholly incapable of any good and prone to all evil." We have to acknowledge, he says, that this depiction does not really "fit with our personal experience, since we encounter all kinds of things that strike us as attractive in the lives of people who are alienated from any kind of faith and in whom we cannot assume regeneration." But then he goes on to observe that the doctrine of common grace allows us to resolve that seeming conflict. "Incapable of any good, and prone to all evil," he says, is a formula that "expresses how each human being, apart from regeneration, would prove himself to be if common grace did not keep his evil impulse in check." The doctrine of total depravity "acknowledges what lies in our depraved nature and what would immediately proceed from us as soon as God ceased to temper this evil impulse through common grace."[11]

While sometimes using the word "restrains" in describing the option that he chooses, Kuyper does not restrict his view of the working of common grace to an "external" operation. In addition to the leashing-type function of divine providence, Kuyper insisted God also extends "internal" gracious benefits to unregenerate human beings. His list of examples is significant here. We see common grace at work, he says, "wherever civic virtue, a sense of domesticity, natural love, the practice of human virtue, the improvement of the public conscience, integrity, mutual loyalty among people, and a feeling for piety leaven life."[12]

Those sorts of things are not just *traits* that we admire in people—we also have reason in many cases to admire the *people* who manifest them. A Hindu mother stays up several nights in a row caring for her sick child. That is a "natural love" that is to be admired—but we also admire the woman who demonstrates it. In the civil rights era, men and women who professed no religious commitments were martyred in the cause of registering black voters in areas where white supremacy was rampant. They are to be honored as individual persons for their self-sacrificial sense of public conscience. In those instances God chooses not only to accomplish positive things *through* the unredeemed but he also does so by working *in* them. He doesn't just hold them back with an external leash—he *un*leashes something in their inner lives to produce things in which he, God, can take delight. And we should take delight also.

The Unavoidability of the "Meta"

It is important to be aware of the kind of choice at stake here—and especially about the fact that it *is* a choice. Furthermore, the choice has to be informed by some broad-ranging considerations.

In his now-classic 1981 book on ethical theory, *After Virtue*, Alasdair MacIntyre made what is for me an intriguing proposal about what must go into testing the full adequacy of an ethical perspective. Every "moral philosophy," he insists, "characteristically presupposes a sociology," which means that "we have not yet fully understood the claims of any moral philosophy until we have spelled out what its social embodiment would be like."[13] What he is getting at is that in addition to engaging in the typical logical analyses of the basic principles of, say, utilitarianism or a deontological ethic, we must also consider what that way of viewing moral matters would look like in a society that lived in consistent conformity to that ethical system.

It strikes me that the same kind of test has to be applied to theological systems. That is exactly what Kuyper was doing, as I read him, in his 1898 Stone Lectures. He was—among other things, of course—sketching out how Calvinism has been, and ought to be, socially embodied. What concrete patterns of cultural interactions have taken shape in the historical development of the Calvinist social imagination? Kuyper was also offering a comparative analysis of how he understands the social embodiments of other theological systems, such as Catholicism and Lutheranism.

I have wondered on occasion what it would have been like if Herman Hoeksema had been elected mayor of Grand Rapids or if Cornelius Van Til had served as governor of Pennsylvania. In thinking about these scenarios, I have had difficulty actually seeing them in these public roles. It isn't because their Calvinist theology as such makes it difficult; Kuyper, after all, was a Calvinist theologian who served in the Dutch parliament, as did Herman Bavinck. And Calvin was actively engaged in public policy matters in Geneva.[14] But the notion of the social embodiment of a theology that sees our non-Christian fellow citizens as the objects of God's undiluted wrath provides a stark contrast to what Calvin and Kuyper advocated.

Nor is it simply about how our different versions of Calvinism view human beings. Our understanding of the character of God is at stake. Here, for example, is Calvin on the biblical mandate about loving our neighbor: the neighbor whom we are commanded to love "includes even the most remote person," extending beyond "the ties of kinship, or acquaintanceship, or of neighborhood." It is a love that should "embrace the whole human race without exception in a single feeling of love," with "no distinction between barbarian and Greek, worthy and unworthy, friend and enemy." And then he adds this punch line: all of these persons, he insists, *"should be contemplated in God*, not in themselves."[15]

It seems obvious that when Calvin encounters the joys and sorrows—and accomplishments—of his non-Christian neighbors, and contemplates those neighbors "in God," he is not inclined simply to issue a verdict of "guilty, foul creatures" in the service of a Lord who "curses all that's foul." These encounters generate feelings of love.

Holding "A Little More"

Charles Spurgeon was aware of the need for making Calvinist "meta" choices. He had made a decisive one, early on in his preaching career, about how to call sinners to turn to Christ. As a Calvinist he believed in what is popularly referred to as "limited atonement"—the teaching that, while the saving work of Christ is sufficient to cover the sins of all human beings, the effective power of that atoning work was meant for only the elect. "All those the Father gives me will come to me, and whoever comes to me I will never drive away" (John 6:37 NIV).

In his preaching, though, Spurgeon would plead with unbelievers to make a decision to come to Christ for saving mercies, engaging thereby in what is known as "the sincere offer of the gospel to all." For this he was consistently criticized by some other Calvinists. How can a preacher ask sinners to accept the benefits of the atonement, they asked, when for all he knows he is preaching to people who are not numbered among the elect?

I love Spurgeon's response to this criticism: "I do not think I differ from any of my Hyper-Calvinistic brethren in what I do believe," he wrote, "but I differ from them in what they do not believe. I do not hold any less than they do, but I hold a little more, and, I think, a little more of the truth revealed in the Scriptures."[16]

In a public debate I once had with David Engelsma in Grand Rapids—in front of an audience of three thousand on a Friday night!—he speculated that given my views on common grace I likely also endorse "the sincere offer."[17] I confirmed his speculation. Like Spurgeon, I support inviting all sinners to turn to

Christ, while I also endorse the theological teaching associated with the idea of the limited atonement.

Like Spurgeon, embracing both the limited atonement and the sincere offer, I see myself as "hold[ing] a little more" than some other Calvinists. Is that because, as my friend Engelsma suggested in our debate, I get carried away by "feelings"? Yes, I replied to him. But my feelings connect to emotions that I see at work in the Scriptures. The New Testament gives us a vivid account of the "feelings" of Jesus, for instance, as he wept over the city of Jerusalem: "Jerusalem, Jerusalem, you who kill the prophets and stone those sent to you, how often I have longed to gather your children together, as a hen gathers her chicks under her wings, and you were not willing" (Matt. 23:37 NIV).

Including "a little more" in our theology means being willing to affirm deeply grounded convictions without knowing how to explain exactly how they fit together within the system of our beliefs. And that is also the case with affirming both total depravity and common grace. They each have their place within a larger theological perspective that attends to "a little more" than what some other Calvinists are willing to engage.

For Kuyper, of course, what we pay attention to in the operations of common grace is more than a *little* more. His insistence on the "internal" dimension of God's favorable dealings with the non-elect opens up a much larger perspective—one that has both continuity and discontinuity with the views of Calvin on the subject.

8

Resisting an Altar Call

When I was getting ready to write this book, I went back to reread a couple of books by James K. A. Smith. I always enjoy reading what Jamie writes—he is one of my favorite authors. And he is amazingly influential. One of his significant recent contributions, for example, has been to make Charles Taylor's thought accessible to a broad Christian audience.[1] I have been reading Taylor since my graduate school days in the 1960s—when he was the go-to thinker on Hegel for analytic philosophers. "If you *have* to read Hegel," I remember one of my professors saying to me, "then read Taylor. He seems to know how to make sense of all of that stuff."

These days, of course, Taylor has become particularly important for Christians because of his account of what has brought us to our "secular age." Having relied heavily on Jamie's exposition of Taylor's thought, I now say to my students: "If you want to understand Taylor—and you *should* want to—then read Jamie Smith!"

One of my favorites of Jamie's books is *You Are What You Love*.[2] I have been teaching the Augustinian perspective on "misdirected loves" for years, and I have always thought I did it well. Jamie's book, though, has not only given me new insights on the subject but I find it positively inspiring—there are some passages that I read simply because it is good for my soul to do so.

My focus in this chapter, though, is Jamie's book *Awaiting the King*. I liked the book even before I began reading it, simply because of the title. I have worried much in recent years that Christian writing about the *kingdom* often does not give adequate attention to the *King*. So when I first saw the cover of Jamie's book, I uttered a heartfelt "Amen!" After some excellent kingdom books—*Desiring the Kingdom* (2009) and *Imagining the Kingdom* (2013)—Jamie was now focusing specifically on the One whose authority gives shape and content to the kingdom.

My appreciation for the book only increased as I made my way through it, even though there are points where I strongly disagree with what Jamie says on specific subjects. Jamie is an engaging thinker and a splendid writer. I learn from him.

A Dangerous "License"?

I am discussing Jamie here freely because he is my friend. When Jamie joined the philosophy faculty at Calvin College, he contacted me to let me know that he was now occupying my old office there. We became friends, and we have often had friendly arguments—even, on occasion, delightful ones.

One of my favorite exchanges with him took place at a session of an annual convention of the American Academy of Religion. It was not too long after the turn of the century, and Jamie had been invited, as an emerging young scholar, to present a paper about how to engage the larger culture as a

Christian. The planners asked me to be the respondent, and I wrote my response early enough to send it to Jamie ahead of time so that he could prepare his response to my response.

I don't know whether I explicitly accused Jamie of being too "Hauerwasian" or "Yoderian" in my comments, but I do remember criticizing him for going too far in the direction of their "Christ against culture" leanings.

Jamie's response to my response was delightful. He took each of the points that I objected to in his paper and showed that I was criticizing things that I myself had written in the early 1970s, particularly in my first published book, *Political Evangelism*. I think he even said that he saw himself as more "early Mouw" in his thinking than "later Mouw."

The memory of that response by Jamie came quickly to mind as I read the first paragraph of the preface to *Awaiting the King*. He reports there that when he started work on his three-volume Cultural Liturgies series, he had a somewhat different idea of what this third volume would be like. He had originally anticipated doing a study of political theology that would be "something like 'Hauerwas for Kuyperians,' a come-to-Yoder altar call for those who were enthusiastic about 'transforming' culture and affirming common grace." In doing that, he had wanted to encourage a return to a stronger emphasis on the antithesis in Reformed Christianity, with a voice "that says 'No!' to cultural assimilation and political injustice." And right there, in the midst of explaining that, he inserts a parenthetical comment saying that the voice he had hoped to use was one that he had heard "most clearly in Richard Mouw's books from the early 1970s."[3]

I laughed out loud when I read that. I got the coded message. Jamie may have toned down somewhat from, as he puts in that first paragraph, the "antitheticalism" of some of his earlier writings to more of "an emphasis on our common life."[4] But the shift has not moved Jamie any closer to embracing the kind of common-grace theology that I have come to defend. He still wishes I had stuck with some of my earlier views.

As he develops his argument in *Awaiting the King*, Jamie sees the idea of common grace as providing for "a low-grade dispensation of the Spirit" that helps Calvinists to feel confident that they are mitigating "the disastrous effects of total depravity left to its own devices."[5] The basic error here, he writes, is that "this common-grace license treats as 'natural' and 'creational' what is in fact evangelical and ecclesial. Talk of common grace abounds, he says, where a theology of *providence* is lacking." The cultural phenomena that common grace is invoked to explain are more properly thought of as resulting from "the historical legacy of special grace, the remnants of the specifically evangelical influence of Christology, ecclesiology, and the gospel."[6]

There is a lot packed into that brief formulation. And it does have the feel of Jamie's original desire to preach a "Hauerwas for Kuyperians" sermon topped off by "a come-to-Yoder altar call," in which those of us who are "enthusiastic about 'transforming' culture and affirming common grace" will offer up our prayers of repentance.

It will be obvious from what I have written thus far in this book that I am not ready to walk down the aisle. But that does not mean that I sense no promptings of the Spirit in the sermon and altar call that Jamie wants to issue to folks like me.

One theme that certainly does resound in my soul is Jamie's insistence on the importance of the doctrine of providence. I have been arguing in these pages against thinkers who insist that providence—as an "external" restraining of sin—can explain just about everything that folks like me want to attribute to the workings of common grace. But in arguing against that view I certainly don't mean to be denying the importance of taking providence seriously. My objection has to do with how *much* the doctrine of providence can adequately explain regarding what many of us see as evidence for an attitude of divine favor toward the non-elect.

Of course, the Calvinist thinkers who put a strong focus on providence in these matters don't really think that providence by itself can simply explain it all. I have already mentioned that Daniel Strange, working with the basics of Cornelius Van Til's theology of common grace, allows that at least some of the good things that show up in the thoughts and deeds of the non-elect are due to the actual historical influence of special revelation as embodied through the centuries in the believing community. And this comports well with Jamie's formulation, already quoted: that what some of us see as the workings of common grace can better be attributed to "the historical legacy of special grace, the remnants of the specifically evangelical influence of Christology, ecclesiology, and the gospel."

Here too I have no difficulty conceding a role played in history by this "legacy" of special revelation on non-Christian life and thought. A good case in point in my mind is so-called secular feminism. I believe that the gospel introduced significant themes about gender equality into the larger culture—as when the apostle Paul says that Christian husbands and wives should submit to *each other* (Eph. 5:21) and when he tells the early church that not only does the wife's body belong to the husband but the husband's body also belongs to the wife (1 Cor. 7:4). These are apostolic teachings that would eventually undermine long-standing ideas and practices that denied women the opportunity to exercise God-given abilities and talents. The feminist concerns that have emerged in the past century or so, then, are due in good part to the fruition of seeds that were planted in Western culture by the proclamation of the gospel.

I have to confess to a sense of irony that I experience on this point when people accuse those of us who want to engage seriously with feminist concerns of "accommodating" to secular culture. My response is that in some cases we do indeed need to accommodate—or to say "Yes!" to—ideas and causes that show up in the larger culture, because they are in fact a part of an unacknowledged legacy of special revelation.

So the legacy of special revelation and the life of the church does have an influence in the larger culture. But do we have to establish that sort of influence before affirming the worth of every specific thing that we want to affirm in the larger culture? I'm not ready to go that far.

One of the memorable sermons I have heard was from a Grand Rapids preacher, Clarence Boomsma, back in the 1970s, on Jonah on the ship threatened by a storm. He said that there was a dispute there between two parties: a prophet of the true God and a bunch of pagan sailors. If that is all the information we had, he said, and we had to choose sides, we would obviously put our money on the prophet. But in this case, he noted, the pagan sailors were speaking truth when they told the prophet that he was putting them in danger by his own disobedience. Boomsma's memorable punch line was this: sometimes the world preaches important messages to the church. I am happy, then, not simply to reject out of hand what secular activists have to say to us on gender and race matters. It is important to listen carefully lest we miss some good sermons!

Fallen, Yes, but . . .

So I am not ready to walk down the aisle in response to a come-to-Yoder altar call. I have paid a lot of attention to John Howard Yoder's writings in my academic journey. Indeed, in spite of my distress over the scandal that has become widely known of Yoder's abusive actions toward many women, I still have to list his 1972 book, *The Politics of Jesus*, as one of the key influences in my own development as an ethicist.

In the latter part of the 1970s and early '80s, Yoder and I did a rather extensive road show together, and we even coauthored a paper on Reformed-Anabaptist differences, published in an ethics journal.[7] Most of our public dialogues took place in Mennonite settings. (The one time Paul Henry and I invited him to speak at the Calvin College campus, Yoder offended the local crowd—me included!—by saying that when Jesus rejected Satan's offer to him of the worldly political powers, Jesus was basically declaring that he refused to be a Calvinist!)

Anyway, in all of that I was convinced that Yoder was, in fact, quite insightful in identifying the key points where Anabaptists and Calvinists differ. The Anabaptists of the Reformation era, he argued, "out-Calvinist-ed" us Reformed types in insisting on an uncompromising emphasis on the noetic effects of sin. Our foolish minds are so darkened by our sinful rebellion, Yoder argued, that we no longer have cognitive access to whatever aspects of an original creation order might still exist in our fallen world. This means, he insisted, that our only hope for understanding God's will for our lives is to look to Jesus's incarnate redemptive ministry as the clear revelation of what God calls us to be and do as human creatures.

Here is an incident that I have regularly cited in setting forth my own disagreements with Yoder. In a Q&A session on a Mennonite campus, someone asked him if he could state in one sentence the exact disagreement he had with me about the patterns of the larger culture. Yoder responded, "Mouw wants to say, 'Fallen, but *created*,' and I want to say, 'Created, but *fallen*.'"

That captures a fundamental issue. We Kuyperians insist that God built certain cultural capacities and goals into the creation, and we see some of what he originally planned for the creation of humankind showing up in the deeds of unbelievers. And we don't see all of this as being adequately explained in terms of either providence or the legacy of special revelation.

Ancient Pottery

So here is a non-Christian cultural phenomenon that I offer for folks like Jamie to consider. In China, about three millennia ago, talented Chinese artists created "eggshell pottery," paper-thin porcelain vases that were delicately crafted with intricate designs. This was over a thousand years before the birth of Christ, and the method used was itself a refinement of a process of creating pottery that had been around even longer in Chinese culture.

What does God think of those pots and vases? I don't think the production of these works of art is explainable simply in terms of the providential restraint of sin. My sense is that the Lord took delight in the talents of the artists themselves in crafting this pottery and wants us to delight in them as well. Nor is it helpful to think of a special revelation legacy as a determining factor.

On the special revelation topic, there is one possibility that should be mentioned: the idea of a *prisca theologica*—the beliefs and practices of the ancient patriarchs that were brought to many locales by the sons of Noah, and have been preserved in corrupted forms in various tribal memories. I don't completely dismiss this notion. Memories of ancient special revelations can linger on in a collective cultural memory. Don Richardson reports, for example, that missionaries discovered, in a Karen village in Burma, a belief in a God called Y'wa—a deity to whom they sang a "song of hope," in which they proclaimed that "if we repent of our sins . . . and pray to Y'wa, he will have mercy upon us again." Richardson proposes that these beliefs "predate both Judaism and Christianity . . . spring[ing] from that ancient root of monotheism which characterized the age of the early patriarchs."[8]

Well, again, possibly. But I don't see how positing a remnant of theological ideas spread by the sons of Noah helps us understand the merits of eggshell pottery or of, say, the even more ancient cave drawings discovered in Australia, or of the polyrhythmic dances of sub-Saharan Africa. Abraham Kuyper insisted that even in locales where special revelation had no clear influence, God is still working to sustain his cultural designs for the creation, and that seems to me compelling in explaining these cultural products and expressions.

Ordinary Phenomena

But I need to push this one step further. For Kuyper, common grace covers much more than the ideas and artistic products of "high" culture. In discussing various examples of common grace, Kuyper distinguished between "external" and "internal" workings of common grace. I have been arguing in previous chapters that many in the Reformed tradition who have made use of his common-grace theology have focused exclusively on matters that can easily be characterized as "external" workings of God in the lives of the unregenerate. When a brutal dictator, for example, releases some political prisoners in order to persuade the international community to lift some economic sanctions, this seems to be a clear case of a providential restraint of sin.

Kuyper went further than that sort of aspect of common grace by focusing on the ways in which a non-salvific attitude of divine favor is at work also in the *inner* lives of unregenerate persons. And, significantly, his examples touch on much more than works of art, philosophy, and literature. As noted earlier, Kuyper says that we can see manifestations of common grace "wherever civic virtue, a sense of domesticity, natural love, the practice of human virtue, the improvement of the public conscience, integrity, mutual loyalty among people, and a feeling for piety leaven life."[9]

Take "natural love." Our plane lands at an airport, and we go to the baggage claim. Three children are holding up a hand-made banner that says, "WELCOME HOME, DADDY. WE ARE PROUD OF YOU!" Some adults are gathered behind the kids, eagerly watching the passengers coming down the escalator. A collective shout goes up when a soldier in uniform steps off. His left arm is in a sling. The children run to him, and he embraces each with his good arm. He stands to accept his wife's embrace. They both are sobbing. I hear someone from behind utter the word, "Afghanistan." I turn to see that like me, he too is blinking away tears.

I have no idea whether this reunited family is Christian. And in that moment the question is not an important one to me. I am moved by what I see. Am I simply being influenced by emotion? Yes—and I think God is too. As the husband and wife embrace, the little boy (about three years old) is clinging to the soldier's leg, crying "My daddy! My daddy!" Is the Lord looking at that child as an object of his eternal hatred? Is God irritated with me for being moved by what I see? Or is God himself taking delight in the touching display of the sort of "natural love" that he originally planned for his human creatures?

An Expansive Calvin

In insisting that mere external restraint in the lives of the un-redeemed is not enough to account for the workings of common grace, Kuyper could find much support in John Calvin's writings. We need to be clear about the fact, of course, that both Calvin and Kuyper do make much of the "external" restraint of sin. In order to keep depraved sinners from doing the worst that they can accomplish, Calvin says, God on many occasions "merely restrains by throwing a bridle over" their sinfulness, holding it in check without doing anything to "purge it within."[10] Kuyper would certainly endorse that.

But for each of them there is more. One of Calvin's apt illustrations of the "internal" workings of common grace falls under Kuyper's "civic virtue" label. The Reformer compares two public leaders in ancient Rome, Camillus and Catiline, noting that each of them as a pagan has to be viewed "under the universal condition of human depravity." But it is also clear, he says, that we must acknowledge that they are different from each other. Catiline clearly engaged in wicked behavior, whereas, by contrast, we can see "endowments resplendent in Camillus [that] were gifts of God and seem rightly commendable if judged in themselves." These gifts, the Reformer insists, were "not common gifts of nature, but special graces of God, which he bestows variously and in a certain measure upon men otherwise wicked."[11]

To be sure, Calvin goes on to stipulate that while the sorts of gracious gifts on display in the public service of Camillus rightly "have their praise in the political assembly and in common renown among men," they will not be counted in the last judgment as having had any "value to acquire righteousness."[12] But Calvin still insists that these virtues we see operating in the lives of the unredeemed are praiseworthy, when "judged in themselves." He is being clear that God is not merely providentially restraining Camillus, but that the Lord in this case wants us to see Camillus himself as a virtuous person.

In an essay published in the *Princeton Theological Review* in 1909—translated from the Dutch by Geerhardus Vos of the Princeton Seminary faculty—Herman Bavinck exposited the Reformer's theological basis for this kind of positive assessment of the "inner" lives of non-Christians. For Calvin, Bavinck says, there is in fallen humanity "still a clear mirror of the operation of God, an exhibition of His manifold gifts."[13] Indeed, Bavinck observes, Calvin speaks glowingly of "a remarkable sagacity [that] is given to [unredeemed] men whereby they are not only able to learn certain things, but also to make important inventions and discoveries, and to put these to practical use in life." And this "sagacity," Bavinck observes, is a product of the working of the Holy Spirit.[14]

We can ask, of course, how it is that the Holy Spirit works in the inner life of a Camillus, creating virtuous dispositions without also regenerating his inner being unto eternal life. Our answer, though, will have to make much of the idea of mystery. Nor is this an embarrassment for a Calvinist, since we should not expect less mystery regarding the workings of common grace than we clearly acknowledge in the regenerating work of the Spirit.

On the latter subject, the Canons of Dort make the case for mystery with eloquence: "This grace of regeneration does not treat men as senseless stocks and blocks, nor take away their will and its properties, neither does violence thereto; but spiritually quickens, heals and corrects, and at the same time sweetly and powerfully bends it."[15] It seems clear that in their understanding of the Spirit's workings of common grace, Calvin, Kuyper, and Bavinck do not see ancient pagans—and, we can add, Chinese potters and reunited families at baggage claims—as mere "stocks and blocks" but also as persons whose "will and its properties" are preserved in producing that which on occasion brings delight to the Lord.

9

A Shared Humanness

"Nothing human is alien to me." A professor had quoted that line in class when I was a college freshman. He attributed it to Ralph Waldo Emerson. It struck me at the time as a profound thought, so I wrote it on a note card and taped it to the wall above my desk in my dorm room. Later I found out that it was from the ancient Roman poet Terence. My professor must have come across Emerson quoting Terence somewhere.

I don't know what happened to that note card, but I do remember thinking about the quotation a couple of years later when I had begun reading extensively from Cornelius Van Til's writings. Having absorbed Van Til's antitheticalism, I wondered whether my earlier fondness for that line was naive. If there are really two kinds of humans, elect and reprobate, then Emerson—who rejected orthodox Christian beliefs—surely fell into the latter category. While it could still be a good thing to study him, shouldn't I be aware that what he claimed as fundamentally "human" was in reality "alien" to the redeemed mind?

As I immersed myself in further studies, I became less Van Tilian in my outlook. I was learning too much from people who were not Christians to see what they were teaching me as nothing more than a catalog of erroneous thoughts.

Years later I was pleased to discover that Abraham Kuyper explicitly endorsed the point that Terence had made: "Humanity is one. . . . It is a mighty trunk with leafy crown. . . . Belonging together, living together upon the same root of our human nature, it is one flesh and one blood, which from Adam to the last-born child covers every skeleton and runs through every man's veins. Hence the desire for universal philanthropy; *the claim that nothing be alien to us that is human*; the necessity of loving our enemy and of praying for him, for he [our enemy] also is of our flesh and of our bones."[1]

As we saw earlier, Van Til accused Kuyper and Bavinck of not being consistent in following through on their basic Calvinist theological convictions. This "mighty trunk" theme from Kuyper would be an obvious case in point that Van Til would direct us to in substantiating that assessment. Fair enough. But we should at least be clear that Kuyper was not unintentionally drifting in a non-Calvinist direction in holding to what Van Til saw as an unfortunate inconsistency. Kuyper unapologetically proclaimed the move he was making as guided by his Calvinism.

To repeat a comment from Kuyper that I quoted in a previous chapter, Calvinists, he says, must make a basic choice: "Either [we] surrender our confession of the deadly character of sin, or hold on to that confession with all our might, but then also confess along with it that there is a common grace at work that in many cases restrains the full, deadly effect of sin."[2]

The acknowledgment of sin's "full, deadly effect" was important to Kuyper. He always insisted that his views on common grace must be held alongside a clear recognition of the reality of "the antithesis," the deep opposition between redeemed and unredeemed patterns of life and thought. His strong emphasis on Christ's rule over all of creation was always tied for him to the deep conviction that the only remedy for sin, both individual and collective, was the atoning work of Jesus Christ.

As Henry Stob put it in an insightful reflection on the antithesis, "When the creature took up arms against the Lord, the universe was split and a cosmic discord reigned, a discord born of and marking the presence of sin. In that situation God stood on one side, and on the other stood the demons and fallen human race indulging in a vain and self-defeating hostility to the Lord of all. The creature warred against the creator; evil against goodness, darkness against light."[3]

The fall, Stob argues in a good Kuyperian fashion, brought about a fundamental redirecting of the human will, away from God instead of toward him. But also in a good Kuyperian manner, Stob insists that while our rebellion against the Creator perversely affects the totality of our human desires and values, "it does not cancel [our] humanity." Indeed, Stob argues, what makes the antithesis between our sin and the will of God "possible at all, is a nature or constitution which is held in common and fully shared by the parties which are set against each other in the cosmic struggle." Thus "the physical, psychological, and mental powers" that are given to us in our original creation as bearers of the divine image are still, by common grace, "distributed indifferently to all, and neither belief nor unbelief significantly diminishes or enhances these natural powers, or alters their common operation."[4]

Underlying the very real differences embodied in the antithesis, then, is our shared humanness. But how do we nurture this sense of humanness in the Christian community? This is no small concern, especially these days as we wrestle with the continuing presence of racism and ethnocentrism in our present culture.

That kind of concern was very much on Kuyper's mind. And with good reason, since he knew that Calvinism has its own unique tendencies toward positing deep divisions within the human race, the most obvious having to do with the insistence upon profound differences between the elect and the non-elect—differences that have frequently been used to counter any tendency to entertain notions of a shared human solidarity.

Kuyper insisted that while the bond that holds the Christian community together "is much stronger, firmer, and more intimate" than the broader human bond, Christian "unity is not independent of the fellowship of nature, but added to it." This means, he argues, that we must be careful to recognize the "*double* root of fellowship." What we should be experiencing *within* the Christian community is the second part of the "double work of the Holy Spirit," which should also be "causing our hearts to be drawn to all that belong to us by virtue of our *human* kinship."[5]

Kuyper regularly focuses on this more general sense of kinship in formulating his Christian approach to issues of public policy. This focus is nicely on display, for example, in an 1891 speech that I discussed in an earlier chapter: his address to the first Christian Social Congress. When Kuyper spoke there of the Savior's compassion for the poor, he was not referring simply to the "believing" poor. In the miracle of the loaves and fishes, Kuyper says, Jesus has compassion upon hungry people, "*even though as yet they do not hunger for the bread of life*." Seeing their physical need, the Savior "breaks the loaf into many pieces and gives them an abundance of precious fish."[6]

Kuyper used this biblical example to highlight the fact that God has a genuine empathy for the concerns of very real individual people, elect and non-elect alike. And Kuyper also knew that this broad-reaching empathy does not always come easily to Calvinists. So Kuyper paid attention to how it can be intentionally *cultivated* in specific ways. He expressly emphasizes the ways that our worshiping life can do some of the work here.

Kuyper argues that a good place to start is in our confession that we belong to "a holy catholic church." What we need here, he says, is a proper understanding of the scope of this confession by allowing the Spirit to expand our awareness of not only the universal church but also the humanity that exists beyond the boundaries of the believing community. The "communion of saints," when properly understood and experienced, he says, "opens its arms as wide as possible."[7] And having learned to open wide our arms in worship, we can go from that root of our specifically Christian fellowship to the broader root to which our Christian identity is inextricably connected: the root of our shared humanity with all who bear the divine image.

I think Kuyper would have liked what the Catholic bishops at the Second Vatican Council said in the opening paragraph of their document *Gaudiam et Spes*, adopted toward the end of the council in 1965: "The joys and the hopes, the griefs and the anxieties of the [people] of this age, especially those who are poor or in any way afflicted, these are the joys and hopes, the griefs and anxieties of the followers of Christ. Indeed, nothing genuinely human fails to raise an echo in [our Christian] hearts."[8]

The bishops are giving expression there to the same emphasis on empathy that we find in Kuyper. The God who responds in mercy to the "griefs and the anxieties" of suffering human beings calls us to do so as well. But Kuyper would also have liked the way the bishops insist that the "genuinely human" that God cares about also includes "the joys and hopes" of humankind in general. The God who grieves over our wounded humanness is also the God who continues to take delight when contemplating the cultural efforts of the unredeemed.

10

The Larger Story

The neo-Calvinist theology of culture begins with creation. God fashioned a world in which human beings would serve his will by doing all things to his honor and glory. When the creation came to be inflicted by the cursedness brought about by human rebellion, God initiated a renewal plan that centered on restoring a portion of humankind for obedience to God's original purposes for the human community, so that men and women could again contribute to the flourishing of created reality in accordance with God's original designs.

God's plan for human obedience in both creation and redemption is not merely for "maintenance" functions. For the neo-Calvinists, humanity is called to engage in a complex creative project of its own, one that furthers God's own creative purposes.

God's desire in this regard is clear in the calling of Israel to be his covenant people. The Creator did not allow the willful rebellion of his human creatures to obliterate his original design for the created order. Looking down on a wayward and broken humanity, the Lord chose a specific people, the tribes of Israel, to be the initial agents of his renewing purposes in the world. Essential to their status as his elect people, God gave Israel complex instructions about how to fulfill his original plan for the creation. They were to show the nations of the earth what it means for a people to farm in obedience to his will; to marry and procreate; to carry out the necessary economic transactions; to configure the political and legal aspects of their collective lives; to engage in art, architecture, worship, and recreation—all as ways of embodying what it means "to glorify God and to enjoy him forever."[1]

The neo-Calvinist movement, as represented by the thought of Abraham Kuyper and Herman Bavinck, insists that the doctrine of common grace has to be firmly grounded in what Jochem Douma describes as "an unfolding of a panorama of cultural history."[2]

The Cultural Panorama

Of course, for Kuyper and Bavinck this "panorama" is itself grounded in the more basic Calvinist vision of God's sovereign grace in bringing individuals to himself. But they also insisted on going on to a next step. God is not only sovereign over the processes of individual salvation; he is also the sovereign Lord over the cultural patterns that have resulted from collective human activity. The business of cultural formation is central to God's purposes in creating human beings. Nor has this diminished in importance under fallen conditions. In a world that is distorted by sin, redeemed people must seek to bring all areas of human life into conformity to the Lord of creation.

The Lord who claims all of culture as a part of his kingdom also calls his redeemed people to show forth his divine rule in the patterns of their own cultural involvement. Here the standard Calvinist discussions of divine election are extended to an emphasis on the divine intention in electing people to eternal life: that believers who have been elected by sovereign grace are thereby called to participate in the life of a redeemed community of believers who together must find ways of bearing witness to the sovereign rule of God over all things.

The Biblical Drama

The neo-Calvinist approach to culture presupposes a rather complex narrative in which the biblical plotline features an original creation, a fall into sin, a redemptive plan that focuses first of all on Israel and then comes to fulfillment in the person and work of Jesus Christ, and the new creation that will be ushered in by Christ's return.

The first stage of the plot is crucial to the rest of the way we neo-Calvinists tell the story. Cultural activity is no peripheral concern in God's designs for his creation. The Creator's initial assignment to the first human pair is a cultural mandate. The directive to "fill the earth" (Gen. 1:28) is not to be thought of primarily as a reproductive command. The "filling" of the earth is a *cultural* activity. God placed Adam and Eve in a garden—raw nature—and told them to start *doing* things in that environment.

When our first parents fashioned tree branches into rudimentary tools, or when they invented a basic labeling system, or when they created schedules as a means of organizing their lives—in all of this they were developing the cultural potential of the original creation as a means of fulfilling their original mandate from God.

The centrality of cultural formation has not been in any way diminished by the entrance of sin into the creation. Under fallen conditions the question becomes one of cultural obedience versus cultural disobedience. Rebellious humanity distorts and perverts cultural activity. This can be seen clearly as the Genesis story unfolds. In the pre-fallen state, technological innovation was a good thing. It was one of the ways in which human beings lived out their mandate to glorify God in all that they do. But when, in Genesis 11, sinful people decided to "build ourselves a city, and a tower with its top in the heavens" so as "to make a name for ourselves" (v. 4 NRSV), we have a clear example of technology gone awry.

To be redeemed from sin, then, is to be restored to the patterns of obedient cultural formation for which we were created.

A Biblical Grounding?

I find all of that convincing. But throughout my years of setting forth various aspects of this perspective, I have kept running into intelligent Christians who were not convinced. These thoughts come across to them as somewhat speculative, as picking up on a few biblical concepts and constructing a rather abstract theology of culture that seems somewhat removed from the actual biblical text. Can we really get as much mileage as we Reformed types want out of a reference in Genesis to "have dominion"?

In the final analysis, of course, the argument comes down to the question of how this culture-affirming perspective comports with the larger biblical message. Does the Bible encourage us to participate actively in cultural activity—art, business, entertainment, sports, education, and much more? And, even more, does the Bible not only call for an active cultural formation on the part of Christians but also encourage Christians to learn from and take delight in what is going on beyond the scope of the believing community? Or has our fallen condition so corrupted God's original intentions for human life that apart from redemption not much good can happen in the realm of culture?

I set out in the 1970s to address this question directly by paying close attention to some biblical passages. I decided to focus specifically on verses dealing with the "end-time," taking my initial hint in writing a book on the subject—which I later revised and expanded[3]—from Revelation 21, which points to the glorious future that God promises to us. In that end-time scenario, the apostle John is given a vision of a new heaven and a new earth, with "the holy city, new Jerusalem, coming down out of heaven from God, prepared as a bride adorned for her husband" (v. 2). Among the many details the apostle provides is this one: that "the kings of the earth will bring their glory into it. . . . They shall bring into it the glory and the honor of the nations" (Rev. 21:25–26).

This passing mention is an echoing of a similar reference in Isaiah 60, where more detail is provided. The ancient prophet foresees a transformed Jerusalem in which "the glory of the LORD has risen" (v. 1). Into this city will come "the wealth of the nations," accompanied by a procession of "kings to the brightness of your rising" (vv. 3 and 11). The "wealth" includes camels from other countries, transporting precious metals (v. 6). Flocks of sheep from what are now the Muslim lands also make their appearance (v. 7). The much-acclaimed wood from the trees of Lebanon—used there to decorate pagan temples—will now be used to beautify the sanctuary of the true God (v. 13). The "ships of Tarshish," vessels carrying the products and materials from many national cultures, will bring their cargo into the city (v. 9). And all of this will now serve the purpose of bringing glory to the Lord.

The greatest promise for our future as believers is, of course, the gathering in of followers of the Lamb from many tribes and nations. But there also seems to be an important gathering-in of the accomplishments of human culture. That which took place as cultural development outside the boundaries of the believing community will also be claimed for the kingdom. This expectation is grounded in a fundamental biblical claim: all authority and expertise in the universe comes from a sovereign

God who holds all people accountable for how they use his gifts. This includes the gifts that are on display in sculpture, music, painting, drama, scholarly production, family life, and the rituals of our communal life, as well as in political governance and economic activity. It all belongs to God—"the earth is the LORD's and the fullness thereof, the world and those who dwell therein" (Ps. 24:1). People may not know that they are exercising gifts for which they are accountable to the Giver, but the Lord will conduct a final accounting. The "wealth of the nations" and the cultural "honor and glory" of the peoples of the earth—all of this will be gathered in at the end-time. And God alone will be glorified on that day.

Once we acknowledge the basic biblical claim that God is the sovereign Ruler over all things, we cannot help but also acknowledge the practical implications. God cares about art, athletics, education, business, politics, and entertainment. All that has been accomplished in human history in promoting beauty, goodness, justice, stewardship, and even that which has flourished in contexts where the name of Jesus has not been lifted up—all of this will be revealed in the end-time as counting toward the coming of his kingdom. To be sure, much of it will need a final cleansing, a purging of all that falls short of the full glorifying of God. But it will be gathered in.

I have been especially taken with what I see as Bavinck's edifying manner of linking this eschatological gathering-in of the cultural riches of nations to the doctrine of the image of God. He insisted that not only is each human individual created in the divine image but there is also a collective possession of the *imago*. The creation of humans in the divine image in the Genesis creation narrative, Bavinck observes, "is not the end but the beginning of God's journey with mankind." In mandating that the first human pair be "fruitful and multiply," Bavinck says, God was making it clear that "not the man alone, nor the man and the woman together, but only the whole of humanity together is the fully developed image of God," for "the image of God is much too rich for it to be fully realized in a single human being, however richly gifted that human being may be." Furthermore, this collective sense of the *imago*, he argues, "is not a static entity but extends and unfolds itself" in the rich diversity of humankind spread over many places and times.[4]

For Bavinck, this understanding of the image necessarily takes on an eschatological significance, when in the end-times "all the glory of the nations will be brought" into the new Jerusalem.[5] "Tribes, peoples, and nations all make their own particular contribution to the enrichment of life in the new Jerusalem. . . . The great diversity that exists among people in all sorts of ways is not destroyed in eternity but is cleansed from all that is sinful and made serviceable to fellowship with God and each other."[6]

For our present-day discussions, this suggests that we might think of the Creator as having distributed different aspects of the divine likeness to different cultural groups, with each group receiving, as it were, a unique assignment for developing some aspect or another of the divine image. And we today have new opportunities to learn from these assignments, in anticipation of the eschatological gathering-in of the peoples of the earth, when many tribes and tongues and nations will be displayed in their honor and glory in the new Jerusalem—and we will then see the many-splendored *imago dei* in its fullness.

Is that "speculative"? Well, maybe a little bit—but only a little bit. It is certainly enough to convince us that God cares deeply about such things as goodness and beauty. This means we also must care deeply about such things—in anticipation of a day when not only the results of active lives of conscious obedience to the will of God but also ancient Chinese pottery will be gently and lovingly carried through the gates of the new Jerusalem.

11

But Is It "Grace"?

I have been offering what I see as plausible grounds for the belief that God uses the unredeemed to do good things and even looks with divine favor on the unredeemed people who accomplish those good things. But I need now to face the question that has been posed by some folks who acknowledged the reality of these good things. Yes, okay: an attitude of divine approval of sorts—but is it really *grace*? Should we not reserve the term "grace" for God's *salvific* dealings with human beings?

Creational Hospitality

I once mentioned to Neal Plantinga, a gifted theologian who served for nine years as president of Calvin Theological Seminary, how much I liked Christine Pohl's study of hospitality in her book *Making Room*.[1] He had also read the book with great appreciation, and we talked about the theological implications of the case that she made. Pohl had pointed out that these days the word "hospitality" has been robbed of its original core meaning, which had to do with making room for people when we are under no obligation to do so. She complained about how the "hospitality industry" is all about "hotels and restaurants which are open to strangers as long as they have money or credit cards."[2]

I told Neal about how I was using her idea of "making room" as a theme for spiritual and theological matters, urging Christians to provide space for ideas, concerns, and questions that we would not otherwise engage. Neal liked that application, but he then proposed a more basic theological appropriation of the "making room" motif. "Did you ever think of this?" he asked me. "God's creating the world was itself an amazing act of hospitality. God did not need us in order to be God." But God "made room" for a marvelously complex creation. And that marvelously complex creation included the likes of us, inviting human creatures into a special kind of relationship with him.

I found that to be an intriguing insight. And this notion of God deciding to "host" a creation fits nicely with Reformed theology. God is God—he did not need a creation in order to add more "being" to himself. Calling the cosmos into existence was a sovereign act of divine freedom.

And, of course, that same sovereign freedom is at work in the other great event of divine hospitality: the incarnation. Sending the Son into the world was a magnificent "hosting" event. Jesus came to "make room" in the very heart of God for the likes of us. As the writer to the Hebrews puts it: "For we do not have a high priest who is unable to empathize with our weaknesses, but we have one who has been tempted in every way, just as we are—yet he did not sin" (Heb. 4:15 NIV). Jesus made our temptations and sufferings his very own.

A Hospitable Creation

The theological move I will make now seems obvious to me. Properly understood, providing hospitality is an expression of grace. In that sense, "gracious hospitality" is a redundancy. In my childhood I learned in catechism that "grace" means "unmerited favor." If hospitality is making room for someone who has no basis for expecting or demanding that we make room, there is always a strong element of grace in genuine hospitality.

Suppose I suggest to someone that we meet at a restaurant to talk about some important topic. The person responds by saying, "No, come to my place. I will make lunch for us. I make a mean grilled cheese sandwich!" And when I tell him that I really don't want to inconvenience him by having him prepare a meal, he responds, "I know I don't really *have* to! But I *want* to do it." This is a perfectly ordinary way of offering hospitality as *unmerited favor*. The host is being *gracious*.

Neal Plantinga was right, God did not "really *have* to" create a world. But he did. And in doing so, he was making room for the likes of us. God was initiating a project in which we finite human creatures could enter into the life—the fellowship—of the divine Trinity.

But it isn't just about us. God made room for all the other creatures described in Psalm 104: storks, wild goats, and trout. And God also made room for the enjoyment—by him and by us—of ancient Chinese eggshell pottery, along with poems, arias, situation comedies, and livable dwellings.

Again, all of this came about as a result of the decision of a sovereign God to make room for a complex creation. That was the understanding of divine hospitality that Neal was getting at. And now I will add to what he observed—but I am not pinning this additional claim on him—that *creating the world, then, was itself an act of grace*. Again, creation was not ontologically necessary. Nor was it a moral requirement—as if it would have been a moral defect for God simply to have decided to be God, without adding "Creator" to his list of titles. The decision to create a world was an act of unmerited favor.

Grace or "Grace"

In 1959 Henry Van Til, nephew of Cornelius Van Til, published an excellent survey of neo-Calvinist thought, *The Calvinistic Concept of Culture*, in which he saw the Kuyperian perspective as clarifying themes that had already been present in Augustine, Calvin, and other Reformed thinkers of the past. He clearly did not share the kind of negative take on Abraham Kuyper's views on common grace that his uncle had set forth.

In this regard, Henry Van Til gave a straightforward affirmation of what he describes as the "beneficent goodness of God to the non-elect sinners." He did express some theological nervousness, though, about using the term "grace" to designate this mode of divine favor. Is it legitimate, he wondered, to link this beneficence so closely to the salvific "blessings which God bestows upon elect sinners in and through Jesus Christ, the Mediator?" Having expressed his misgivings, Van Til stuck with Kuyper's label—but he did say that he preferred "to place the term 'common grace' in quotation marks."[3]

In my earlier book on common grace I endorsed Henry Van Til's expression of caution. "We do well," I said, "to heed Van Til's misgivings about any talk of common grace that does not put at least mental quotation marks around the word 'grace.'"[4] While I see no reason to retract that word of caution now, neither do I see any reason to reissue it with any passion. I think Van Til was willing to go along with the term—albeit with mental quotation marks—because that was the label that had come to be associated with Kuyper's theology, and he realized that challenging the adequacy of the label could detract from

Kuyper's laudable purposes. He decided that since Kuyper had made "common grace" the preferred label for his view, it is better, all things considered, not to change it.

I have now come to be more confident regarding Kuyper's use of the term "grace" than I was when I wrote my earlier book on the subject. I think it is a fine term, with no quotation marks needed. If grace is unmerited favor, then I am convinced that God's unmerited favor extends beyond that which is manifested in his saving mercies toward individuals.

Going back to my expansion on Neal Plantinga's creation-as-hospitality theme: if God's decision to create the world is itself an expression of unmerited favor, then there is a graciousness at the heart of God's relationship to created reality itself.

None of this would have struck John Calvin as theologically strange. Jochem Douma observes that John Calvin did "not just sporadically characterize God's gifts to the Gentiles as 'grace.'" Calvin did so with much frequency, and he also used alternative terms—"blessings," "love," "benevolence," and so on—to describe God's positive assessment of the thoughts and deeds of the non-elect.[5]

Douma also points out that there is "a yet broader application" of the idea of grace in Calvin's thought—his insistence that divine grace was at work even in pre-fallen humankind.[6] But Calvin's application of grace goes even a step further. Douma finds Calvin treating the nonhuman creation itself as serving as an object of God's grace. Here Douma quotes a comment that the Reformer makes with reference to a verse in the book of Nahum: even "the mountains cannot remain standing in their own strength, except as far as they are supported beneath by the grace of God." Indeed "the world [itself] cannot for a moment remain standing except as far as it is sustained by the grace and goodness of God."[7]

I can imagine some folks insisting at this point that the concept of grace is being extended too far, even if the extending is done by Calvin himself. While I side with the Reformer on this, I do have some sympathy for the worry that is just beneath the surface of the objection. When we start talking in our theology about God extending his grace to the Alps, have we not moved pretty far away from the fundamental theological and spiritual impulse that led to the *sola gratia* of the Reformation?

One of my favorite novels is *The Diary of a Country Priest* by the early twentieth-century Catholic writer Georges Bernanos. In the final scene the protagonist, a French country priest, is dying, and his friend apologizes to him that a fellow priest will not arrive in time to administer the last rights. The priest replied: "Does it matter? Grace is everywhere."[8]

I find that line compelling, especially when I give it Calvin's interpretation. God not only stays relationally near to his creation but also at each moment he is holding all things together by his sovereign will. God, being God, did not need—ontically—a finite creation. But he chose to call the cosmos into being. He graciously—hospitably—made relational room for the creation. The implication of John 3:16–17 seems obvious: God did not just *make* the cosmos—he *loves* what he has made. God loves the Alps, then, as he graciously sustains them at every moment.

The "grace is everywhere" line should not be affirmed, though, without maintaining a clear focus on the marvelous saving grace that is *not* everywhere. In the midst of fallen humanity, God has by his electing mercies called out a people to show forth his glory. The patterns of the life of redemption do stand over against the ways of rebellious humanity. The antithesis is real, and neo-Calvinism cannot flourish without staying focused on that reality. We need to give some attention now to why that is so.

12

Attending to the Antithesis

In his *Dutch Calvinism in Modern America*, James Bratt describes the emergence of two opposing theological parties that took shape among those Dutch Calvinist immigrants who drew upon elements of Abraham Kuyper's theology. He labels the parties "positive Calvinist" and "antitheticalists."[1] Both parties shared the Kuyperian insistence on forming "separate organizations" in a variety of cultural spheres, but they disagreed on the larger *purpose* of such organizations. The antitheticalists saw the formation of Calvinist schools and labor unions, for example, as a necessary way "to strengthen antithetical consciousness,"[2] whereas the positive Kuyperians, Bratt explains, viewed the formation of separate organizations as a training ground and platform for engagement with the larger culture.

It will not surprise anyone who has read thus far in this book that I am on the positive side of this polarity, but not without some significant qualms. In describing the motivation of the positive Kuyperian party, for example, Bratt says that it was their desire in advocating sphere-related separate organizations "not to shelter the elect from the world but to prepare them to go out and transform it."[3] I have worries about two words in that brief description. First, I am not happy about the implication that the antitheticalists were driven simply by a concern to "*shelter* the elect." That is too disparaging. The cosmic struggle between the forces of righteousness and unrighteousness is real, and being clear about the struggle is serious stuff. Our engagement with the larger culture requires careful spiritual discipline in discerning the spirits (see 1 John 4:1).

Second, I am wary about calls for Christians to go out into the larger culture to "*transform* it." The transformation of cultural life is, I am convinced, an eschatological reality. We must take on the present challenges of Christian discipleship with a *vision* of the ultimate transformation of things in Jesus Christ. We *await* the day when all things will be made new. To be sure, our waiting must include active efforts to be obedient to that vision—doing what we can with the gifts available to us to address the opportunities that come our way. Sometimes we will be able to see initial signs and firstfruits of the final transformation. But the emphasis must always be on obedience, not on transformational "victories."

The article "Of the Last Judgment" in the 1561 Belgic Confession is both instructive and inspiring in this regard. There is coming a day, it says, when "the faithful and elect shall be crowned with glory and honor; and the Son of God will confess their names before God his Father, and his elect angels; all tears shall be wiped from their eyes; and their cause, which is now condemned by many judges and magistrates as heretical and impious, will then be known to be the cause of the Son of God."[4] Those words were written, of course, by Christians threatened by severe persecution. But the basic point applies to our own broader engagements. To be faithful, even in what may seem to be insignificant areas of our lives—by discerning what it means to be obedient to the will of God in our workplaces, our classrooms, in serving the poor, and in what we enjoy in stadiums and museums—these things will be revealed someday as having contributed to "the cause of the Son of God."

The great missionary-theologian Lesslie Newbigin put it well:

> We can commit ourselves without reserve to all the secular work our shared humanity requires of us, knowing that nothing we do in itself is good enough to form part of that heavenly city's building, knowing that everything—from our most secret prayers to our most public political acts—is part of that sin-stained human nature that must go down into the valley of death and judgment, and yet knowing that as we offer it up to the Father in the name of Christ and in the power of the Spirit, it is safe with him and—purged in fire—it will find its place in the holy city at the end.[5]

Keeping a Focus on the Antithesis

Those of us who endorse common-grace theology need to be aware of the need to keep certain tendencies in check. While there is no obvious reason to think, for example, that a strong emphasis on common grace inevitably leads to theological liberalism, we need to be aware of how common-grace thinking can move people in that direction. Indeed, it has actually done so.

Here is a case in point that I have written about elsewhere. Quirinus Breen died a few years before I joined the Calvin College faculty in 1968, but some of my older colleagues admired him as a distinguished Calvin alumnus—which he was. After his Grand Rapids studies—college and seminary—he was ordained as a Christian Reformed minister in 1920, at a time when common grace was a much debated topic in the midwestern Dutch Calvinist community. Breen was an ardent supporter of the Kuyperian perspective. But even though common-grace theology won out in the denomination with the 1924 affirmations, Breen began to resent the fact that the Christian Reformed theologians continued to emphasize the necessity of also supporting the idea of the antithesis. He eventually transferred his credentials to the mainline Presbyterian denomination, and after doctoral studies he went on to have a distinguished scholarly career, most of it spent on the University of Oregon's history faculty.

Breen came to emphasize the need for a theological understanding of God's dealings with humankind "as inclusive as the generosity of divine charity could make it." These inclusive impulses led Breen to commend the likes of the Beat poet Lawrence Ferlinghetti and the artist Pablo Picasso as "the church's sons," as prophetic voices who serve the Christian community faithfully as they "devote themselves to knowing the truth about man and his actual attitudes to himself, to other men, to nature, [and] to the mysterious forces beyond man's control."[6]

I don't want to make this one case bear more theological weight than it deserves. But it does serve as a significant reminder to me personally about what can happen when the neo-Calvinist theology of common grace comes to be disconnected from the doctrine of the antithesis. To repeat Henry Stob's description of the depraved condition that was initiated by the rebellion of the fall: "The creature warred against the creator; evil against goodness, darkness against light."[7]

Antithetical Mindfulness

The dangers of downplaying the reality of the antithesis are real, and they must be acknowledged. How do we protect ourselves from those dangers? One remedy is to stay aware of the *importance* of the antithesis. For enthusiastic proponents of common-grace thinking, this requires effort in order to avoid tendencies that may pull us in wrong directions.

I am convinced of the importance of the "tendency" factor in theology. People who emphasize divine sovereignty in the process of salvation tend to go in certain directions on other theological matters, while those who emphasize our free choices go in other directions. Those who stress the unity of the Godhead tend toward modalism, while those who focus on the three-ness tend toward social trinitarianism—and in each case other theological topics are affected.

Earlier I mentioned the idea—inspired by an observation from Alasdair McIntyre about ethics—that a theological system has a corresponding sociology. The past debates in the Christian Reformed community about the point of having separate sphere-related organizations were clearly connected to questions about social identity. Calvinist immigrants engaged in heated arguments about these matters while they were struggling with questions about their role in North American culture. And because each side sensed their respective theologies had significant social implications—one dominated by common grace and the other by a strong emphasis on the antithesis—they tended (I use that word advisedly) to avoid sounding like they were conceding anything important to the other group's theological formulations.

So I acknowledge the personal need to be mindful of the antithesis because I am aware of tendencies to take common grace in wrong directions. And here is where I go for the help I need to sustain that mindfulness: I make myself pay attention to the antitheticalist camp. In these pages I have discussed Cornelius Van Til, Daniel Strange, Herman Hoeksema, and David Engelsma—and, yet to come, Klaas Schilder. I reread these theologians recently, but not just because I was writing this book. I regularly check in with their writings to keep myself engaged with the challenges they pose to my way of viewing things.

For me, as a person who spends quite a bit of time reading and rereading theological works, that is an effective way of imposing the discipline upon myself. But there are other ways we can also explore. Maybe we common-grace types need, for example, a devotional book that includes daily antitheticalist readings and prayers!

13

Religions Now
"More Precisely Known"

During the past decade or so in my speaking and writing about non-Christian religions, I have gotten a lot of theological mileage from a comment that Herman Bavinck makes in the first volume of his *Reformed Dogmatics*. For much of the Christian past, he observes, "the study of religions was pursued exclusively in the interest of dogmatics and apologetics." From that perspective, "The founders of religions, like Mohommed, were simply considered imposters, enemies of God, accomplices of the devil." This assessment no longer holds, Bavinck says, because now those religions "have become more precisely known" from what we have been learning from "both history and psychology." And then Bavinck offers this theological verdict: "Also among pagans, says Scripture, there is a revelation of God, an illumination by the Logos, a working of God's Spirit."[1]

Again, I have gotten some good mileage from using these insightful comments from Bavinck, particularly in what I take to be the robust trinitarian structure that he employs in describing the kind of "revealing" that we can discover in non-Christian religion. Given Bavinck's explicit reference to "Mohommed" in setting forth this structure, for example, we can take Bavinck as encouraging us to expect to find in Islam not only "a revelation" from the First Person of the Trinity but also an "illumination" by Christ as the Logos, as well as a "working" of the Holy Spirit.

The use of a trinitarian formulation here by Bavinck suggests the need for some new thinking by neo-Calvinists about non-Christian religions. Bavinck's allusion to the Father's revelation in nature is standard fare in Reformed thought, but it carries no assurance that those to whom God is doing the revealing actually "get" what is being revealed. As Jochem Douma points out regarding John Calvin's thought, for example, the Reformer "does recognize a general revelation," but this does not lead him to posit a natural theology.[2] The major Reformed confessions, in outlining God's creational revelation, quickly add that the natural mind is not capable of making any good use of the revelation, which leaves unredeemed persons "inexcusable" (Westminster Confession, chap. 1) and "without excuse" (Belgic Confession, art. 2) in their unbelief.[3]

If those statements about general revelation are all we have, then the status of other religions is obvious. God reveals something true to them, but they do not effectively appropriate that truth. To put it crudely: God puts it out there for them, but he knows that it will do them no good. The function of general revelation is mainly to hold them "without excuse."

By bringing the other two persons of the Trinity into the picture, though, Bavinck gives us a more complicated scenario. The Son provides persons in other religions with an "illumination," and the Spirit is "working" among them. This raises two obvious questions, then: What, for example, is the divine Logos *illuminating* in the hearts of persons in non-Christian religions? And what is the Spirit intending to accomplish in *working* in their lives?

Let me say right off that I do not see Bavinck making a claim about a positive *salvific* status for persons of other faiths. But he is clearly encouraging a more charitable approach for us in engaging in dialogue with other religions. I will explore what this means for us by using Islam as a primary example.

Knowing the "More"

Significantly, Abraham Kuyper clearly shares Bavinck's perspective with reference to Muslim life and thought. In Kuyper's lengthy reflections on his firsthand encounters with Islam during his Mediterranean tour—now available in an English translation—he expresses fairly strong admiration for Muslim life. Especially interesting is Kuyper's observation about the character of Islam's founder. "By what magic," Kuyper asks, "did Mohammed radiate such an unparalleled charisma" that his "imprint is still very evident" even in the "remotest areas" of the Middle East? Kuyper cannot believe that the Muslim prophet was simply engaged in "a deliberate act of deception." Religious perspectives that are set forth by leaders who want to deceive their followers, he says, have no sustainability. "Charlatans live a lie," says Kuyper, and typically "even the highly-polished brilliance of the visionary's luster is quickly extinguished and does not provide the staying power that governs the centuries." Muhammad, in contrast, seems to have possessed a "spiritual power of the first order," and even if there were "factors of a lower order" also at work in extending his influence, the primary force was "the power impelling his spirited and resilient call for monotheism."[4]

Kuyper argues in this connection that what sustains a genuinely religious vision—and here he continues in the spiritual-psychological vein—is that it "stirs the deepest longings within our very being, more powerfully than any other single factor through the passage of one's personal life and throughout the history of humanity." The power of Muhammad's vision resides "in his deep conviction of the sinfulness of polytheism and in his robust confession of monotheism."[5]

But Kuyper also admired something else in Muhammad's perspective: the Muslim founder's awareness of the need to "give structure to his confession," insisting that the recognition of "the all-encompassing supremacy of Allah's omnipotence [be] stretched as a net over all of human existence. And this extended equally over all aspects of life—personal and domestic, social and political."[6]

Thus the parallel to the case for Calvinism that Kuyper had recently set forth in his Princeton lectures: a compelling religious vision is one that takes hold in human hearts, forming a community that eventually gives shape to that vision in the form of sustainable structures in a broad range of societal life.

Kuyper's firsthand impressions of Islamic culture comport nicely with Bavinck's more general observation that we are in a better position these days than were our forebears to explore our relationship to other religions because these religious systems have "become more precisely known" to us. And this "more" to which we now have access is provided to us, he says, by "both history and psychology."

What kinds of things did Bavinck have in mind when he said that historical and psychological factors now provide new insights into Islam and other religions? And how does the consideration of these factors revise in significant ways what we would come up with if we look at these religions exclusively from dogmatic and apologetic perspectives?

It is obvious, of course, that on a very practical level we know a lot more these days about Islam than Kuyper and Bavinck did. While Kuyper had to travel around the Mediterranean in order to encounter Muslims firsthand, we do not have to journey very far at all. We have Muslim neighbors. They are our fellow citizens. Some of us have Muslim friends, and in some cases Muslims are even members of our extended families. All of that certainly brings to us some new "knowing" about Islam—as does the awareness of threats posed by acts of terrorism and serious political tensions in the Middle East.

One thing that those of us engaged with North American evangelicalism surely also know these days is that offering any kind of positive observation about Islam's religious vision can stir up controversy. And it seems obvious that both Bavinck and Kuyper were indeed offering positive assessments of Islam on specific points.

Of course, neither Bavinck nor Kuyper was ignorant of anti-Christian patterns of thought and action on the part of the Muslims of their day. What Kuyper and Bavinck were insisting upon, however, was that the very real existing tensions between Christianity and Islam not be seen as a barrier to deeper theological probing. And with reference to this kind of deeper probing, I do not have the impression that we have moved much beyond Bavinck and Kuyper in our assessments of Islam. But I am also convinced that we do need to keep at the task.

Unfallen Diversity?

The need for the further probing that we must take was impressed upon me at a small gathering in 2011 at Calvin Theological Seminary, where a few of us "senior scholars" were invited to interact with some PhD students working on neo-Calvinist topics in their graduate research. My particular assignment was to respond to an excellent—and for me, very stimulating—paper by Jon Stanley, then a student at Toronto's Institute for Christian Studies.[7] In his paper, Stanley argues for an exploration of "the contours of a distinctively neo-Calvinist theology of religions," insisting that neither the founding generation of our movement, nor those of us who have worked on expanding the overall project for our contemporary context, have managed to come up with a robust theological perspective on the plurality of religious worldviews in the twenty-first century.

Stanley argues, as a case in point, that there is a serious inadequacy in the typology that Sander Griffioen and I had developed in our 1993 book *Pluralisms and Horizons*,[8] particularly in our threefold distinction among *directional, associational,* and *contextual* pluralisms. Stanley does not object to the way we identified and characterized these as distinct types. Rather, he insists that questions of multifaith realities are not clarified by utilizing *only* these types. Thus his proposal for adding a fourth type, which he labels *confessional* pluralism.

Stanley was on to something important in raising this concern. Griffioen and I had attempted to portray the variety of religious worldviews in terms of the antithesis between belief and unbelief, and that rubric does work fairly well, as Stanley notes, with reference to those worldviews—Freudianism, Marxism, Enlightenment humanism—that fix upon some aspect of the created order, such as the psychic, or the political-economic, or human rationality—as the reference point for explaining all of reality. Non-Christian perspectives, we argued, are either directed toward the worship of the God who sent Jesus into the world or they direct their ultimate trust within the creation.

What Griffioen and I were not focusing on explicitly, however, was the "thickness" of non-Christian religious systems of life and thought. And given the strong emphasis in many religions on that which is beyond the natural—the realm of the transcendent—it is surely inadequate simply to see such worldviews as putting their ultimate trust in some aspect of creaturely existence.

Stanley was eloquent in making his complaint about neo-Calvinist thinkers—and he had Griffioen and myself in mind in making his point—who assume that religious plurality can simply be contained within the "directional" category. These thinkers will fail to assess the gifts to be found in other religions, he says, "no matter how robust their doctrines of common grace, how nuanced their view of the antithesis, how complex their social theory, how appreciative they are of various relative religious goods in non-Christian religions, how respectful they are of religious expression in the public square, and how open they are to learning from other religions and the religious other (even the outright idolater)." To be sure, he quickly adds, these are "all things, of course, to be lauded." But they are not enough.

Again, I take this challenge seriously. We do need something more in assessing other religions than what our standard neo-Calvinist accounts of directionality, common grace, and antithesis have provided. As I was writing this book, for example, someone posted on a Facebook page the comment that all non-Christian religions are manifestations of "idolatry." I posted a reply asking whether he was convinced that an Orthodox Jew who daily prays the psalms of David is engaging in "idol worship." His response: "Of course!"

I am not convinced of that. At a consultation on Islam someone asked an African theologian—who had testified about coming to faith in Christ after being raised a Muslim—whether he saw his conversion as having come to worship a different God. He smiled and said that his personal experience in his prayer life as a Muslim was that he and God were characters in a black-and-white movie, but that when he came to Christ suddenly the movie had been dramatically transformed into living color.

I have heard similar testimonies from converts from Judaism. They talk about having seen the God of the Bible from a great distance, while they now see him more closely in the face of Jesus Christ. Our theological formulations need to wrestle with those very existential claims about how God is understood in the context of the conversion experiences.

To admit that generic talk about "other religions" ignores the unique character of Judaism and Islam still leaves us with the task of exploring these unique features without thereby slipping into a lowest-common-denominator approach in comparative studies of religious plurality. Cornelis van der Kooi has made this point in a compelling way in his discussion of the habit these days of grouping together Christianity, Judaism, and Islam under the rubric of "Abrahamic religions." He does not deny that the Spirit of God can be at work in those other religions, but in attending to that fact, he insists, we must be sure to focus on the unique identity of each religion. It is not enough, van der Kooi says, to look for commonalities that trace back to Abraham. Christians must also focus on "going forward to Jesus Christ and to thinking and living out of Him" in order to stay true to "our basic [Christian] ideas of incarnation, kenosis and substitution."[9]

That "going forward" sense of Christian identity strikes me as essential to a neo-Calvinist theology of religions. I do not think, though, that this rules out our viewing Islam in particular in terms that go beyond the range of common grace—there is a significant family connection with the Muslim faith that we do not share, for example, with Hinduism.

Kuyper was obviously aware of the dangers that van der Kooi points to. Islam, he says, makes a "fatal error" in rejecting the Jesus of the New Testament, placing "a false prophet above him."[10] Significantly, though, that critical comment about Muslim belief occurs in a meditation on the story of Hagar, where Kuyper offers some of his most poignant comments about Islam.

He sees it as significant that Hagar and her son Ishmael—whom Kuyper saw as the father of the Islamic nations—plays a role in the Bible's redemptive narrative. Given the biblical attention to that role, says Kuyper, for Christians the Muslim religion, for all of its errors, "remains enveloped in mist." Because of Islam's refusal to see Jesus for who he really is, Kuyper says, Muslims "remain stranded in the Old Testament," closing themselves off from "the fulfillment of the New."[11]

That is not something that we could sensibly say about Hinduism or animism. It does make sense for Christians to depict Judaism as "stranded in the Old Testament," and Kuyper wants to see Islam as sharing that condition. And this certainly means for him that our conversations with Jews and Muslims will differ significantly from those with representatives of other world religions. Kuyper's common-grace theology, then, encourages us to seek to cultivate a case-by-case hermeneutic for discerning particular manifestations of God's favor toward people in other religions.

Missiology and the Spirit

The need to discern the uniqueness of different religious perspectives has been at the heart of the missiological focus in recent decades on the need to be aware of cultural *context* in bringing the gospel to diverse peoples. Much of this has, of course, been articulated with reference to evangelizing and discipling persons from other faith communities. Speaking about the gospel to animists will require attending to different matters than when we are engaging in evangelism in Muslim or Buddhist contexts. To be sure, theology of religions must surely attend to more than missiological topics. But neither should the sensitivities that have emerged in missiological explorations be ignored.

The missiological focus on specific contexts has often been guided by the conviction that the Holy Spirit is present in those contexts and may in fact be using unique cultural—including religious—aspects of those circumstances to prepare people for the reception of the gospel. This way of viewing things requires, then, detailed attention to a cultural context as a unique opportunity for discerning how the Spirit may be at work in a specific set of circumstances.

In acknowledging the importance of recognizing the ways in which the Holy Spirit is at work beyond the boundaries of the community of Christian believers, we must never lose sight of the fact that the mission of the Spirit is indeed linked intimately to the good news about Jesus. There are parts of the world these days, of course, where actually speaking to others about that good news is not an easy thing to do. Indeed, new difficulties are emerging in this regard even in cultures where the gospel has had a prominent influence in the past.

But it helps much to know that we are not on our own in witnessing to the power of the gospel. Kuyper's common-grace theology assures us that the Spirit is working "internally" in many lives beyond the borders of the church. Our task, then, in our interfaith encounters is to discern how the Spirit may already be at work in the deep places of the souls of those with whom we are conversing.

And whether we are thinking primarily about the Spirit's role in the workings of saving grace or broadening our attention to the function of the Spirit in common grace, we cannot lose our focus on what is central to the mission of the Spirit wherever the Spirit is at work. The Holy Spirit points human beings to Jesus Christ. In regenerating sinful human hearts, the Spirit brings people to place their trust in Jesus alone as the one who did what we could never do for ourselves, by taking upon himself the dreadful burden of our guilt and shame on the cross of Calvary.

Jesus Christ is also at the center of the Spirit's mission in the operations of common grace. Jesus is the one who holds all authority in heaven and on earth. The renewal of culture in this present age is a preparation for the day when he will return to make all things new. The great cultural eschatological vision of the final gathering in the honor and the glory of the nations is about a grand procession into a city that "does not need the sun or the moon to shine on it, for the glory of God gives it light, and the Lamb is its lamp" (Rev. 21:23 NIV). The goal of the Spirit's common-grace mission will finally be realized when the victory song of the Lamb who was slain is sung.

14

Common Grace and "the Last Days"

When I was asked by a neo-Calvinist friend how my book—this one—on common grace was coming along, I told him that I was presently focusing on the "Bible prophecy" aspects of the topic. "What in the world does Bible prophecy have to do with common grace?" he asked.

I was not surprised by his reaction. Neo-Calvinists typically do not focus on topics associated with Bible prophecy. Not that our movement has generally ignored theological eschatology as such. The new creation that will be ushered in by the return of Christ is obviously a crucial element in the neo-Calvinist scheme.

But Bible-prophecy types have typically focused primarily on events leading up to the time when all things will be made new in Christ. Finding clues to what will happen in the world leading into "the end-times" has been a major pastime for many evangelicals. I worked for two summers in my teenage years at a Bible conference where I heard much about how, for example, in Ezekiel 38 "Gog and Magog" refers to twentieth-century Russia, "Meshech" refers to Moscow, and "Gomer" stands for Germany.

I was skeptical at the time about what I was hearing, mainly because I had been warned by some Reformed friends that some of the theology I would be hearing at the Bible conference would be questionable. Later on, I came to grasp for myself the Reformed basis for avoiding those speculations.

The neo-Calvinist movement has avoided this kind of speculation by following the mainstream of the Reformed tradition in adopting an amillennialist perspective, where the thousand-year reign of Christ described in Revelation 20 is seen as a symbolic portrayal of the kingly rule of Christ that was initiated in a special way by his death and resurrection. By denying the future-event character of the millennium, speculation about other possible "last days" events is also seen as theologically unnecessary by many amillennialists.

Having experienced the excesses of Bible-prophecy scenarios, I find amillennialism to be theologically refreshing. But I have often puzzled about the wholesale rejection of any last-days interests on the part of amillennialists. Does our amillennialist denial of a future earthly thousand-year reign of Christ rule out seeing other last-days references in the Bible as historical events that are yet to come? In this regard it is refreshing for me to find that both Klaas Schilder and Abraham Kuyper insist—for somewhat different reasons in each case, but both from within an amillennialist perspective—that a proper understanding of the unfolding of God's cultural purposes in history requires attention to specific events that will happen in the last days before the return of Christ.

I'll make some comments about Schilder first, starting with several general comments about his theology of culture. This is a good point at which to give him some credit for his contributions to neo-Calvinist thought.

Cultural Abstention

First of all, Klaas Schilder *is* a neo-Calvinist. I have to say that because he is sometimes actually seen as a strong critic of neo-Calvinist thought. Indeed, that was my initial impression when I first read his short book *Christ and Culture* in the mid-1990s. I had been sorting out my various disagreements with Stanley Hauerwas at the time, and in reading Schilder I had the sense that I had come upon an early-twentieth-century Dutch Calvinist version of Hauerwas. For example, Hauerwas had famously argued that "the first social ethical task of the church is to be the church,"[1] which means, he explains, that the church best serves the larger culture when it "sets its own agenda. It does this first by having the patience amid the injustice and violence of this world to care for the widow, the poor, and the orphan."[2]

And now here is what I found Schilder saying: "To establish *koinonia* in the *sunousia* [his term for our shared humanness], as members of the mystical union of Jesus Christ, that truly is Christian culture."[3] Living our faithful commitments in our family life, taking our daily work assignments seriously, serving the needs of our own church members—these things, writes Schilder, are "worth more in potential [cultural] force than a complete academy of science that has not seen God."[4]

Schilder, however, does endorse much of the Kuyperian framework. Indeed, he is credited with coining the term "cultural mandate."[5] A refusal to take that mandate seriously, he says, "means not serving God in what belongs to him."[6] Christ is indeed for Schilder the Lord of all culture, which means that Christ's followers must submit to his lordship in all aspects of life.

Taking the mandate seriously, however, does not mean for Schilder that we must simply act on that mandate. Indeed, he argues that under present conditions the church's calling has to be "abstinence" from attempts at cultural renewal outside the boundaries of the life of the church. In advocating for cultural abstinence Schilder does not want believers simply to ignore the problems that plague the larger human community. Schilder has very harsh words for the kind of "Christian [cultural] abstinence" that "originates in resentment, laziness, diffidence, slackness, or narrow-mindedness";[7] such, he says, "is sin before God."[8] What he is calling for, he says, is a "heroic" abstinence,[9] and this happens when believers are so busy "maintaining their colleges, supporting their missionaries, and caring for the needy who were left them by Christ, . . . [and] are doing a thousand other works of divine obligation" that they do not have the time to perform those highly visible works of "cultural transformation" which Kuyper and others have seen as obligatory. Schilder underscores his point here by citing "Matthew 19:12, where Christ speaks about those 'that make themselves eunuchs for the Kingdom of heaven's sake' and not in order to avoid this Kingdom."[10]

Historical Context

Schilder's call to cultural abstinence is closely linked to his pessimism about the culture of his own time and place. That negative assessment was certainly shaped by the Nazi occupation of the Netherlands—he was even held captive for a while for his outspoken resistance to Hitler's minions. But he was convinced that an even greater crisis was yet to come. And this is where he gets specific about last-days matters. We are presently living, Schilder contends, in an "interim-of-the-interim" period of human history. The larger interim began with the curse of the fall and will end at the return of Christ. The present era, however, is a shorter interim within that larger interim. This shorter interim began, Schilder argues, at the end of the era when the larger culture was not yet as anti-Christian as it is in the present, and it is moving toward an even more aggressively anti-Christian cultural situation than we presently experience.[11] All we can do for now is to cultivate the "self-development of God's people" to live faithfully in anticipation of the day when "the war will be over."[12]

It is important to note that there is nothing here about a general pattern of cultural unfolding in history—the kind of emphasis to which Kuyper is given. Schilder's views about our present historical context are mostly of an empirical nature. He looks at the characteristics of cultural life in a specific historical era, and in the light of that he discerns what the cultural calling should be in that context. And he sees history in our own time as moving into the end-times stage.

Schilder and Kuyper do not really disagree about what the cultural status quo will actually be like in the time immediately before Christ's return. But Schilder, unlike Kuyper, does not rely on a conception of an overall developmental process in making his case. As Jochem Douma puts it, "Schilder does not give us a philosophical history of culture, in which culture gradually reaches its culmination." Rather, for Schilder, in our fallen world "sin snaps the blossoming of culture and, as a result, we receive only cultural fragments."[13] And in our present era, for Schilder, the church has to produce the kinds of cultural fragments that bear witness to God's creating and renewing purposes for humankind—and this in anticipation of a coming crisis when the fragments produced by the redeemed will be pretty much the only positive cultural realities.

The "Lawlessness" Motif

Here is where Schilder makes a very specific biblical identification with an end-times historical figure. The coming crisis will be occasioned, Schilder says, by the appearance of the "man of lawlessness" referred to in 2 Thessalonians 2:3, a major cultural actor who will work closely with the beast whose emergence is discussed in Revelation 13. To take these prophecies seriously, Schilder warns, is to "make believers careful as never before" in discerning our obligations in the larger cultural contexts in which we find ourselves.[14]

Schilder treats this man of lawlessness as a single historical individual who will actually appear on the historical stage. In doing so he is following Kuyper's example. Kuyper had made a detailed case for why the man of lawlessness must be seen as a "distinct individual" rather than a symbolic depiction of "a hierarchical series of persons over a period of more than a thousand years." The spirit of the coming antichrist, says Kuyper, has been "at work long before he appears." But the expressions "'man of lawlessness' and 'son of destruction' are delineated so sharply and defined so narrowly that we denigrate the clear wording of Paul's testimony if we do not think here of a single individual."[15]

Kuyper makes it clear on this that he is departing from standard Reformed patterns on end-time topics. Indeed, he blames the mainstream Reformed interpreters of the past for reacting too strongly against premillennialism—he uses the term "chiliasm"—on these matters. Because of "a one-sided reaction against chiliasm," he says, Reformed theology "had reached a point of permitting Maranatha on our banner of faith to fade in a culpable manner." It is appropriate, then, to "praise and thank divine sovereignty that chiliasm has directed us Reformed Christians again forcefully and passionately to that Maranatha." Not surprisingly, though, Kuyper quickly goes on to warn against allowing the chiliasts "to tempt us to fall into the other extreme." While "the eyes of faith" compel us to hold that the return of Christ "is very near," we must also, Kuyper urges, be aware "that the Lord does not come before the process ordained of God finally ends in the great rebellion and in the gigantic manifestation of the mystery of lawlessness that will incarnate itself in the appearance of the terrible man of sin."[16]

A Lawful Creation

It is not difficult to see why the image of a full display of lawlessness in the end-times would resonate with Kuyper and Schilder. For neo-Calvinism the God of the Bible is very much a legislator. In the beginning, God called forth a lawfully ordered creation. Then sin made it impossible for human beings to discern this law structure clearly. But the coming of Christ has changed things. Kuyper declared this boldly in the Stone Lectures: "Verily Christ has swept away the dust with which man's sinful limitations had covered up this world-order, and has made it glitter again in its original brilliancy. . . . The world-order remains just what it was from the beginning. It lays full claim, not only to the believer (as though less were required from the unbeliever), but to every human being and to all human relationships."[17]

While the "full claim" of the creation order bears on believer and unbeliever alike, this does not mean that the unregenerate consciousness has a clear cognitive access to this ordering. The most that can be said is that unbelievers are accountable for their failure to acknowledge the Creator's purposes. Gordon Spykman summarizes the neo-Calvinist perspective on this matter: "The creation order establishes an ontic commonality and solidarity among all peoples, even in the midst of the radical noetic polarities among differing faith communities."[18]

This conception of God's dealings with his creation is so prominent in neo-Calvinism that when Herman Dooyeweerd and his brother-in-law Dirk Vollenhoven developed their major project of constructing a philosophical system based on Kuyperian insights, they called their system *de wijsbegeerte de wetsidee*—"the philosophy of the law-idea." As Dooyeweerd puts it, this system treats "the conception of the lex as the *boundary* between God and the creation,"[19] so that law is the very means by which God creates and sustains the cosmos.

The Historical Process

There are no obvious differences between Schilder and Kuyper on the fact of a creational law structure. They disagree strongly, however, in their understandings of how the patterns of human history take us toward the end-times crisis.

Schilder has no use for the idea of a common grace that is operative in the unregenerate human community. What keeps unredeemed humanity from doing all the evil they are capable of is God's restraint on the power of Satan. During the course of history, he argues, God restrains Satan, and on some occasions that divine restraint has meant that the blessings that can accompany the proclamation of the gospel even "penetrate very deeply into the circles of the unbelievers."[20] While "this restraint is never completely lacking in this world," neither will it "be constant in measure" throughout the course of time. Indeed, we can be sure, he says, that it "will decrease to a minimum at the end of time," when "any *status quo* existing between the Church and the world will be denounced—from both sides—also in cultural life, even precisely there. Then the whole world—except God's elect—will crowd together around the Antichrist."[21]

Culminating a Process

Kuyper has a similarly gloomy view regarding the events of the end-times, but he insists that the scenario for those concluding days can be properly understood only if we "speak of both a

doctrine and a history of common grace."[22] The form that
the terrible manifestation of sin will take in the appearance of
the antichrist will be produced "precisely by the functioning
of common grace," says Kuyper. "The lawlessness would in
any case have manifested itself terribly, both with and without
common grace, but only common grace gives it this refined
form."[23] It is precisely because of the workings of common
grace in history that the end-time will be characterized by an
utter lawlessness!

This final manifestation of that lawlessness comes about in
this way: throughout history, "common grace has increased
man's intellect a hundredfold." This means, in turn, that the
achievements of unregenerate humanity came increasingly to
take on the form of "an atheistic system," resulting in a general
"godless theory of life" that ultimately "glorifies man and bans
all faith."[24] And the end-times culmination of this process is
realized when "the self-deification of man has become absolute;
and in the end the fruit of this refined sinful development is
ripe, and only then can it happen that the full-blown result of
this process will ultimately be embodied in the person of one
all-powerful human being, and that mighty, all-dominant man
will be the man of sin, the son of destruction." This thoroughly
evil person will then "turn the whole power of the world against
Christ and his people and his church." When this happens, "a
further delay of the final judgment would therefore be meaning-
less, [and] the Christ of God will then end the drama of world
history, destroy the man of sin by the Spirit of his mouth, and
appear himself gloriously in all his saints."[25]

Common Grace and Sphere Sovereignty

The major difference between the two accounts of what leads
up to the end-times is clear. For Schilder, as things move toward

the final stage of history God radically decreases the providential restraints on sin, while for Kuyper the cultural potentials that were built into the original creation will in the end-time "ripen" through the operations of common grace—to the point that fallen humankind finally will be possessed by a spirit of absolute self-deification.

In one sense, then, we seem to be faced with a choice between these two scenarios. For those of us who accept Kuyper's version of the *doctrine* of common grace, we have to take seriously also his account of the *history* of common grace. This history, in turn, is closely aligned with another Kuyperian account regarding the history of cultural development—namely, that which is associated with his doctrine of sphere sovereignty.

In Kuyper's scheme, the diverse spheres of cultural interaction —family, art, politics, economic activity, and the like—are the results of a process of sphere differentiation. We Kuyperians often illustrate this process with reference to the *tribe*, which originally came upon the scene as an undifferentiated cultural entity: the tribal chief is the leader of a kinship system but also has authority over economics, the military, cultic religious practices, the arts, the games, agriculture, and the like. As history has further developed, however, these spheres have become differentiated, with each sphere exhibiting its own unique functions and patterns of authority. The family differs significantly in this regard from an art guild, or an athletic team, or a local business. (On this view, a "family business" combines, say, the authority structures of two different spheres—and the effort often demonstrates the awkwardness of failing to be clear about sphere differentiation!)

Schilder was not impressed with what Kuyper offers as the biblical basis for sphere sovereignty. He argues that Kuyper moves much too quickly from citing the "according to its kind" of the Genesis creation account to the positing of a variety of cultural spheres, each with its own unique authority structure.

To go from the fashioning of specific animal species to arguing for diverse patterns of cultural interaction is, Schilder insists, "a rather large leap"—much too large to serve as the basis for Kuyper's contentions.[26] Schilder was right about this, of course, although my own sense—which I have spelled out elsewhere[27]—is that a Kuyperian-type rationale for diverse creational spheres can be developed if we take care to fill in the necessary theological moves that Kuyper himself does not provide.

End-Time Differentiation

Peter DeVos, a philosophy colleague at Calvin College, once suggested a sphere-sovereignty scenario to me that I continue to find compelling. The historical process of sphere differentiation, he observed, leads to increasing fragmentation when viewed as a "horizontal" time line. There was an integral unity that characterized, for example, tribal identity. When the various functions and authority patterns separate out into differentiated spheres, it can promote a sense of fragmented selfhood. On a personal level, what does my role as a wage earner mean for my role as husband, church member, citizen, participant in leisure-time activities, and so on. From what resources do I draw upon for a sense of integrated selfhood?

Pete had a clear answer to that question: for Christians the sense of integrated selfhood comes from acknowledging the person of Jesus Christ as the ruler over every sphere. The same one who is Lord of family life is also Lord of economic and political life. "He is before all things, and in him all things hold together" (Col. 1:17). The believing community strives toward the integration of our lives by engaging in the continual process of seeking a communal discernment of the will of Christ for our lives by submitting to the authority of his Word.

But, Pete observed, in the larger culture where people do not acknowledge the rule of Christ, the process of differentiation leads to increased sphere fragmentation. And then, Pete suggested, the time will fast approach when the differentiation process culminates in an ultimate fragmentation. At that point in human history, when it appears that everything will simply fall apart, Christ will return to make all things new.

There is a convergence of this sphere differentiation scenario with the insistence of both Schilder and Kuyper on a literal interpretation of the man of lawlessness prophecy. If the only real remedy for the fragmentation resulting from complete sphere differentiation is to be found by putting our trust in the person of Christ, then it makes sense that the unredeemed will ultimately look to a person—an *anti*-Christ—to fill that void. This person will seduce fallen humanity with false promises of integration by claiming for his own person the absolute authority that belongs to Christ alone.

The Importance

Abraham Kuyper's depiction of a very real man of lawlessness who will appear in the days immediately prior to the return of Christ is not a mere incidental theological addendum to his theology of common grace. It is an essential feature of his theology of culture. Whether he has it exactly right in interpreting the Pauline reference in terms of a single historical individual who will appear in the last days, or whether the reference should be taken as a type that is instantiated to various degrees in specific historical figures, we must certainly take Kuyper seriously in his warning that there are dangerous times coming.

I take Kuyper's warning personally. In a memoir-type book I wrote, I reflect critically on the fact that much of my teaching and writing throughout my career has been motivated by a desire to find common ground with people with whom I disagree on some important matters.[28] And I see this as a clear indication, I wrote, that my theological tendency is to place a stronger emphasis on the common-grace side of things than on the reality of the antithesis. I acknowledged the dangers of that tendency, and I confessed that a key reason why I have continued over the decades to keep engaging the thought of antithetical Calvinists—particularly Hoeksema, Van Til, Engelsma, and Schilder—is to keep being challenged by those who are critical of common-grace theology. I have made this same confession earlier in these pages.

While I continue to see the need for engaging the view of those thinkers, then, it has helped also to discover, in the course of writing this book, the "Bible prophecy" elements in Kuyper's own thought. In insisting on the importance of the man of lawlessness prophecy, Kuyper was incorporating a strong antitheticalist reminder into his own system. A time is coming when the workings of common grace will cease. The antithesis will be, in that time, the pervasive reality. It will be—and here Kuyper issues a terrifying warning—such a troubling time "for God's church on earth, which, if these days were not shortened would even draw the elect along into the apostasy."[29]

None of that negates what we saw John Calvin stating so clearly: that to deny the very real cultural gifts that we can receive from the unregenerate is to grieve the Holy Spirit. As long as common grace is at work in the world, we must honor what it produces. But this requires testing the spirits to see whether they really are from the Lord, for horrific manifestations of evil are yet to come. But that will not be the end of the story. Maranatha!

15

Neo-Calvinism in America

At the beginning of this book I said that one of my *aggiorna-mento*—"updating"—projects is to contribute to the recontextualization of neo-Calvinism for present realities. More specifically, I want to explore what is needed to make Kuyperian thought more accessible for our North American evangelical context. This requires, as I see it, two updating efforts. One is a certain measure of "de-Dutchifying" neo-Calvinist thought. The other is making some of the key themes of Kuyperianism more accessible to the broad evangelical movement in North America.

I will look at each of these projects in this chapter. Admittedly, my treatment will be briefer than they deserve. But I hope that what I have to say on these subjects will at least point the way for others to think in more detail on what is required. I can deliver only some sketches about matters that deserve a more robust historical account.

Kuyper and Presbyterianism

When Abraham Kuyper visited Princeton in 1898 to deliver the Stone Lectures, he clearly saw himself as entering friendly theological territory. And there were good reasons for this expectation. His correspondence with Benjamin Warfield had been cordial, and the one Dutch Calvinist on the Princeton faculty, Geerhardus Vos, was a devotee. More broadly, the Dutch Reformed and the Scottish Presbyterian traditions shared historical commitments to the theology of the Calvinist Reformation, and Kuyper's university and the Princeton theological school were seen as bastions of Reformed orthodoxy. Kuyper's visit, then, could be a significant occasion for exploring how his important cultural project could be de-Dutchified and would translate well into the Presbyterian mission in North America.

And Kuyper began his lectures by expressing enthusiasm for that kind of translation project:

> A traveler from the old European Continent, disembarking on the shore of this New World, feels as the Psalmist says, that "His thoughts crowd upon him like a multitude." Compared with the eddying waters of your new stream of life, the old stream in which he was moving seems almost frostbound and dull; and here, on American ground, for the first time he realizes how so many divine potencies, which were hidden away in the bosom of mankind from our very creation, but which our old world was incapable of developing, are now beginning to disclose their inward splendor, thus promising a still richer store of surprises for the future.[1]

Kuyper then quickly goes on to cite some gifts that Europe has to offer to the American setting: experiences drawing from "a longer historical past," for one thing. But still, he shows much hopefulness regarding the new paths that a vital Calvinism might take on American soil.

There was, however, quite a disconnect between Kuyper and his Princeton audience. His Princeton hearers did not really grasp what Kuyper meant to be telling them. As George Harinck observes, Kuyper's desire to inspire North American Calvinists to launch "a new offensive" in the broad reaches of culture did not have the intended effect. Princeton, says Harinck, simply was not "the right place anymore in 1898" for launching this kind of cultural offensive. The result was that Kuyper's message "did not have any impact in the Presbyterian world at all."[2]

The strand of "Old School" Presbyterian theology that had held sway at Princeton for the previous half century featured a Calvinism in which soteriological and ecclesiological issues were central. And more recently, orthodox Calvinism had been under attack from growing liberal quarters, both in the church and among theologians, and many associated with Princeton were feeling increasingly marginalized in the larger church world.

Kuyper was not clueless about developments of this sort. Just a little over a decade earlier he had performed a key role in a major church split in the Netherlands over similar issues of orthodoxy. Not only had Kuyper come out of that ecclesiastical conflict as the leader of a new and vigorous church movement but he also had much else going for him in Dutch society, including considerable political influence: not long after his American visit he would serve a term as the prime minister. He came to Princeton, then, with a confidence regarding the potential for a Calvinist impact in the broad reaches of culture.

His Princeton hearers, however, were concentrating on different concerns. There were about forty of them in attendance at each of his Stone Lectures, and they were primarily church and seminary leaders whose interests, as Harinck reports, were mainly in "the domains of church and theology." Thus they were not inclined to respond with enthusiasm to Kuyper's clarion call to bold cultural engagement.[3]

119

Their failure to connect with what Kuyper meant to be communicating can be seen in the subsequent uses they made of Kuyper's speeches. The few reviews of Kuyper's presentations were, Harinck observes, "all of a theological nature." Harinck also finds it significant that when J. Gresham Machen quoted from the Stone Lectures at the founding ceremony for Westminster Theological Seminary, Machen used this sentence from Kuyper: "It does not matter if a Reformed church is small, if only it is healthy and sparkling with life."[4] Given that the overall thrust of the Stone Lectures was an affirmation of Calvinism as a broad force for cultural influence, it is significant that this is the one remark by Kuyper that gets lifted up by Machen.

Midwestern Dutch Calvinism

There wasn't much enthusiasm for Kuyper's cultural vision in the Dutch Calvinist immigrant communities in the Midwest. While Kuyper had many admirers in Michigan and Iowa—he visited both areas after his time in Princeton—the Christian Reformed churches and institutions were still struggling to understand their own place in American culture. There was, for example, much resistance at the time to switching to the English language in worship and denominational gatherings.

Soon the Dutch Calvinist immigrants would enter into several years of internal theological controversies. James Bratt has chronicled the wrenching disputes that the Christian Reformed churches experienced in the opening decades of the twentieth century: the departure from the denomination of a small movement of dispensationalists; a major case of a theologian being accused of endorsing "higher criticism"; and the angry debates over common grace that led to a split between Herman Hoeksema and his followers.[5] Not surprisingly, then, during the 1930s and '40s the Christian Reformed community was in no mood for more controversy, and its theologians settled into a pattern that Henry Stob labeled "the mind of safety."[6]

The result was, as Harinck notes, that there was not any significant institutional support for an American neo-Calvinism in the decades between Kuyper's 1898 visit and World War II. "And it is common knowledge," Harinck writes, "that a spiritual movement may be very powerful, but if it does not found institutions as its strongholds, it is difficult to consolidate its influence and it is not likely to last very long."[7]

Newer Influences

As we move to the post–World War II era, the Kuyperian vision begins to take hold in the broader evangelical community. There is much in this recent history that can be written about, but I will make only some brief comments, for two reasons. One is that spelling this out should be done with careful historical nuance, which I cannot provide. And second, I have been a bit too close to some of this to give the kind of balanced account that is needed.

Actually, there is much to be gleaned about this relatively recent history from an insightful personal narrative by Byron Borger, who with his wife, Beth, owns a wonderful bookstore in South Central Pennsylvania. The piece was published online in the Borgers' newsletter,[8] and its coverage of the people and developments in the story of neo-Calvinism's emerging influence in post–World War II evangelicalism ought to be expanded to a book-length historical account.

Byron writes about his youthful days as an evangelical "social justice guy" who got caught up with peacemaking, justice issues, and the first Earth Day. Many of his evangelical elders frowned upon his interests, and he could not find resources in Catholicism and liberal Protestantism—or certainly in new left movements—that satisfied him theologically and spiritually. His early evangelical inspirations came from John Perkins, Ron Sider, biblical feminists, and others.

Then he discovered Kuyperianism, especially from scholars associated with the Institute for Christian Studies in Toronto—a graduate school founded by post–World War II immigrants who also spread the neo-Calvinist word through conferences and publications. The star of Borger's narrative, however, is Pete Steen, a dynamic itinerant scholar-organizer who helped to birth the Coalition for Christian Outreach, a Pittsburgh-based Kuyperian ministry to college students at a variety of secular campuses. This movement did much to make Kuyperian ideas—worldview, sphere sovereignty, the lordship of Christ—accessible to students of evangelical conviction.

Borger goes on to mention other positive developments for a broader influence of neo-Calvinist ideas: Charles Colson's discovery of Kuyper, Francis Schaeffer's best-selling books, and the increasing influence of Kuyperian themes in evangelical liberal arts colleges and universities.

There is much more in Borger's discussion that deserves attention. For now, I will mention two takeaway impressions that I have. One is the noticeable absence in the Borger narrative of any significant references to seminary-based scholarship. Nor is this an oversight on his part. To the degree that there has been a spread of neo-Calvinist thought in recent decades in North American evangelicalism, it has largely occurred in the world of the humanities, the social sciences, and the study of popular culture.

The other impression has to do with Borger's references to the "Dutch accent" that he and many others had to get used to in thinking about the basic issues. Borger does not complain about this. Indeed, he clearly associates that factor with his good experiences of being introduced to new dimensions of Christian thought and action. But it is interesting to think about the degree to which neo-Calvinist thought is linked to, say, a century and a half of intellectual and cultural phenomena in the Netherlands.

Abraham Kuyper and Herman Bavinck developed their pioneering ideas in the context of social and intellectual life in the Netherlands in the nineteenth century, and for many decades their way of viewing things was further developed in the next generation of Dutch thinkers. To write, say, the history of the first seventy-five years of neo-Calvinist thought is to construct a narrative that certainly has a Dutch "in-group" feel to it.

With the extensive translation of major neo-Calvinist works into English, as well as new attention being given to neo-Calvinism by many in the broader Reformed and evangelical communities, it is possible these days for non-Dutch evangelicals to more fully "own" neo-Calvinism in applying the key concepts to our North American context. But to what degree is it essential also to "own" some of the distinctively Dutch influences that have shaped neo-Calvinism, in order properly to grasp the significance of at least some of the key ideas?

While I think that the Dutchness of the system can be kept at a minimum in our present context, it cannot be completely exorcised. Al Wolters has helpfully marked out, for example, what he sees as the philosophical basics that we must retain in Herman Dooyeweerd's thought. We certainly need to explore, says Wolters, new philosophical categories and terminology in our contemporary efforts "to give philosophical expression to the basic neocalvinist vision of life and the world." But what we must preserve at all costs in the Dooyeweerdian legacy is "the philosophical commitment to the constancy of creation, and to creation as delivered by the creator, prior to the Fall, as the normative standard to which creation is being redeemed and restored."[9] That captures the philosophical essentials for me. But in order to be confident that we are properly focused on those essentials, it certainly seems necessary for at least some of us in the North American movement to keep studying the ways that Herman Dooyeweerd and his followers gave systematic expression to those essentials. That will require maintaining at least a little bit of Dutchiness as we move on.

The Common-Grace Connection

The continuing relevance of the Dutch *wetsidee* philosophy to contemporary neo-Calvinism is clearest on matters relating to sphere sovereignty. Since much of what Kuyper and others explored regarding diverse cultural spheres and the importance of sphere-related "separate organizations" (political parties, labor unions) was decidedly European, it is illuminating to look at what was seen by the next European generations as important for providing the necessary philosophical infrastructure.

It is not clear to me how much of that is relevant to current uses of common-grace theology, however. Many of the common-grace discussions during the past century and a half have taken place here in North America, and Dutch Calvinists in the nineteenth century who had recently arrived in the United States wrestled with their relationship to the surrounding culture. As Henry Zwaanstra points out in his history of the immigrant community in that era, it was common for the Christian Reformed theologians to characterize the larger North American culture as intrinsically "Methodist," which for them referred to the pervasive experiential and pragmatist texture of what they experienced in their new environment. They were convinced that a special effort needed to be made to preserve a way of life based on deep "principle"—which, they insisted, meant sticking as much as possible with the Dutch language.[10]

Those immigrants were obviously engaging in a bit of caricature in their use of "Methodism." But they were also motivated by some legitimate concerns about how they fit into the New World. And when, several decades later, they began to debate vigorously about common grace, this had much to do with their changing relationship to American culture. Their past reliance on the Dutch language and on other strategies of ethnocentrism were weakening, with the result that they could not avoid asking what they genuinely had in common with their non-Dutch neighbors. And while some of their theological debates still made use of the Dutch language and referred to Dutch theological resources, the debates were very much about life in the United States. Issues about how properly to assimilate to the surrounding cultural environment were driving their theological arguments.

What I have been arguing in preceding chapters, however, is that the theological formulations that characterized those debates in the early twentieth century were not adequate to grasp the full significance of common-grace theology. On all sides, as I have tried to show, the doctrine of "external" providence was stretched beyond its capacity to explain the "gifts" of the unredeemed. And my proposed remedy, as I have been making my case in these pages, has been in effect a plea to draw more carefully on the Dutch precedents and parallels to the American debates. I have insisted on learning more on the subject from what, for example, Kuyper, Bavinck, and Schilder had written in their very Dutch theological context.

Given all of that, I need now to pay some attention in the next chapter to the question of how *much* of the Dutch theological background actually needs to be acknowledged and preserved for an effective neo-Calvinist presence in present-day North America.

16

How Much Calvinism?

The students whom I taught during my seventeen years on the Calvin College faculty typically had no problem understanding Abraham Kuyper's thought. When I started teaching there in 1968 the student body was over 80 percent Christian Reformed, and many of them had heard about Kuyper at least in the catechism classes of their early teens.

Many of them were eager to use the Kuyperian framework for exploring what it means for the subjects they came to college to study. And there was a lot of interest in questions about how the lordship of Christ would shape the professions they would be entering. There was, of course, the occasional jaded student. One young man from an Iowa farming community expressed resentment about Kuyperian themes. For eighteen years, he said to me with a disdainful tone, he had been hearing farmers talk about "planting corn to the glory of God

126

and all that other 'agricultural mandate' stuff." But he was an exception.

What especially impressed me about those students was that their Kuyperianism was grounded for them in the Calvinist theology that they had absorbed as they were growing up. They understood that Christ was not only their personal Savior but also the Ruler over all creation. They identified themselves as members of the covenant community. And their understanding of the cultural challenges went well beyond a narrow focus on church and state. They were conversant with standard Kuyperian themes: "Every square inch," "Christian worldview," diverse spheres, common grace, "image-bearers."

The Kuyperian Option

When I joined the faculty at Fuller Theological Seminary in the mid-1980s, I was quickly made aware of being in a very different pedagogical environment—and not just because I had moved from an undergraduate liberal arts institution to a graduate theological school. My students came from diverse backgrounds, and they were eager to learn about a variety of perspectives within the broad evangelical tradition. Some of them had cultivated strong social-action commitments before coming to seminary, but often with perspectives shaped by various Anabaptist thought and Barthian influences. Most of them arrived at Fuller knowing nothing about Abraham Kuyper.

I would still assign the Stone Lectures in Fuller courses on theology of culture and social ethics, but always as part of a mix that included John Howard Yoder, Stanley Hauerwas, Dorothy Day, and some liberation theology. I would be candid with my classes about my own Kuyperian commitments, but never with the implication that they would have to align themselves with my views.

During my early years at Fuller there was a lot of talk among seminary-level evangelicals about ministering in a "post-Christian" culture, with corresponding condemnations of the "Constantinian" and "Christendom" patterns that we were now appropriately "post." Many of my students, then, were not disposed to draw wisdom from a nineteenth-century theologian who had also served as his nation's prime minister.

In describing that Fuller context, I am not complaining. I found it exciting to offer the neo-Calvinist perspective as one compelling option for evangelicals who were serious about cultural engagement. And to attempt to make that case in classrooms with students from dozens of nations in the Southern Hemisphere, and also representing diverse denominations and non-denominations (Living Waters Community, Fire-Baptized Fellowship), was for me positively exciting.

There were occasions when the neo-Calvinist perspective clicked with some students. One memorable testimony came from an African American Pentecostal student—a gifted preacher well before she took any homiletics courses. "Reading Kuyper," she said to me, "gave me a gift I have been wanting for years! Yeah, there is some racial stuff about Africa that irritated me. But: 'Every square inch of creation!' He showed me a Jesus who saves me by his blood and then tells me to work for justice! That's going to make me a better Pentecostal!"

I find testimonies of that sort from some of my students to be deeply gratifying. But they also raise significant questions for me. To what degree can the key neo-Calvinist themes—the supreme kingship of Christ, the antithesis, common grace, sphere sovereignty—be appropriated by persons who do not endorse the rich Calvinist system that informed the ways that Kuyper, Bavinck, and other Dutch Calvinists developed these ideas?

"Thick" Confessionalisms

Here is a question that I have posed to some of my neo-Calvinist friends: *Do you have to be a Calvinist in order to be a Kuyperian?*

The question came up for me in a striking way in 2017, when I was a guest speaker at Roberts Wesleyan University. Before I gave my lecture, I was introduced to the audience by Richard Middleton, a faculty member there. I had long admired Middleton's work and considered him a fellow neo-Calvinist. He had done his graduate work at Toronto's Institute for Christian Studies and the Vrije Universiteit and had published some excellent things in the tradition of Abraham Kuyper and Herman Dooyeweerd.

I was taken aback, then, by this line in his introduction: "Like Rich Mouw I am a Kuyperian. But while he is a Calvinist Kuyperian I'm a *Wesleyan* Kuyperian."

I didn't have a chance to quiz him about how he understood "Wesleyan Kuyperian," but I have a pretty good sense of what he meant. The Kuyperian component would basically come down to five themes: Christ's lordship over the whole of created reality, the importance of having a Christian worldview, sphere sovereignty, the antithesis, and common grace. Those five items are certainly *necessary* for being a Kuyperian but, taken together, are they *sufficient*?

Here, once more, Al Wolters offers wise counsel. In his 2005 piece looking back on a half century of North American neo-Calvinism, he stresses the potential contributions that non-Calvinist perspectives can make to enrich neo-Calvinist life and thought. He observes, for example, that many of the North American advocates of the neo-Calvinist system often "paid more attention to the dangers of pietism and its relative neglect of the call to cultural discipleship than to the importance of cultivating genuine piety or authentic spirituality."[1] This has been a defect in the movement, and he calls for a new openness to "the whole range of traditional spiritual disciplines, as cultivated in Protestant, Catholic and Eastern Orthodox circles," as well as the "vibrant biblical Christianity" of Pentecostal and charismatic movements.[2]

Wolters goes on to emphasize the need for neo-Calvinism, also in its substantive philosophical-theological views, to cultivate a more "ecumenical character." And then this important observation: "It seems to me that true ecumenicity will always depend on biblical and confessional rootedness, and not on finding the lowest common denominator. Thus I believe that neocalvinism, if it remains true to its radical original intuition, can truly embrace the riches of other traditions, even as it shares its own with others."[3]

Again, that is wise counsel. I fully endorse a more robustly ecumenical neo-Calvinism. There are still questions, however, about the "Calvinist" component of neo-Calvinism. In our efforts to "embrace the riches of other traditions," do we see ourselves as taking significant insights from the "other" confessional perspectives and integrating them into a theological program that is recognizably *Calvinist*? What of the "confessional rootedness" of Kuyper must be preserved?

It should be obvious that much of what Kuyper thought to be essential to a robust Calvinism is not shared by many present-day neo-Calvinists. Kuyper firmly endorsed supralapsarianism, a commitment not shared even in his own day by his colleague Herman Bavinck. Ecclesiology was a major topic for Kuyper. He represented that strand of Dutch Reformed thought that opposed "hierarchical" views of ecclesial authorities, insisting on referring to "broader" church assemblies rather than "higher" ones—which puts him at odds with many Anglican Calvinists and Presbyterians who accept the ecclesiology of the Westminster Confession. There are Baptist neo-Calvinists who differ with Kuyper's views on the sacraments. Middleton's "Wesleyan

Kuyperianism," of course, pushes us even farther—as do folks many of us know who wed key neo-Calvinist themes to Lutheran and Catholic theological allegiances.

While these pairings raise interesting issues, though, I don't really see them as seriously problematic. The thinker who combines a deep commitment to Catholic doctrines with, for example, an affirmation of sphere sovereignty and common grace has likely done some serious theological work in exploring the ways in which neo-Calvinist ideas can be grounded in non-Calvinist confessional commitments. There is much to learn from those explorations. The cases I worry about are ones where people embrace neo-Calvinist ideas relating to cultural engagement where they themselves do not have much by way of any confessional grounding at all.

Evangelicalism is a coalition movement that subscribes to a consensus set of theological emphases that are captured nicely, as I see it, in what we have come to call "the Bebbington Quadrilateral": the need for a conversion, the Bible's supreme authority, a cross-centered view of Christ's redemptive work, and an active discipleship.[4]

I find those items to constitute an excellent consensus set of doctrinal emphases for a movement that is a coalition of people and groups from a variety of confessional communities. But those doctrines by themselves do not make for an adequate theology. To cite just one factor: there is really nothing about the church in the quadrilateral. That doesn't have to be seen as a defect if we can be confident that those four theological emphases will be undergirded by one of several ecclesiologies that have historically informed the evangelical movement.

The problem these days in evangelicalism, however, is that the convictions represented by those four emphases frequently function as a kind of free-floating "generic" package of convictions with no "thick" confessional grounding. This is a significant problem—indeed, I see it as a serious crisis. I rejoice, then, when I actually come across someone who has decided that the best way to be an evangelical is to explore the ways in which the quadrilateral-type convictions can be strengthened by being grounded in a thick Lutheran or Anglo-Catholic confessional context. And it gets even better for me when such a person also holds to some key Kuyperian themes. The arguments that we might have about how best to ground our Kuyperian notions regarding cultural engagement in a robust theology could surely be healthy for evangelicalism in general.

An Ecumenical Spirit

A Dutch scholar once remarked to me that Kuyper typically did his theology "on the run," regularly adapting theological themes to pressing political realities. The scholar illustrated this in a striking manner. When Kuyper needed his political party to take an unpopular stance on some issues, the scholar said, he would preach the antithesis, and when he wanted to form a coalition he would preach common grace.

That assessment struck me as bordering on caricature. But even as a straightforward accurate report, it does not have to be seen as a negative comment. Theologizing "on the run" is still theologizing. I wish more busy political leaders would know enough theology to do it. But Kuyper also managed to write some excellent theological studies on subjects that were not directly related to the issues that preoccupied him as a public leader. Further on, for example, we will look at his treatment of soteriological topics.

Kuyper was capable at times of an impressive ecumenical openness. He revealed this side of himself toward the end of his Stone Lectures, for example. Having condemned the "naturalistic, rationalistic system of thought" he saw as shaping much of the theology of the day, suddenly his tone shifted. We should not simply condemn liberal theologians who deny Christ's divinity, he said. Many of them genuinely want Jesus to "continue to glitter from the throne of humanity, as the highest ideal of the modernized human heart." Thus, warned Kuyper, the Calvinist "who would look down upon such men, would only dishonor himself."[5]

At that point Kuyper also went on to soften some of the harsh assessments he had made earlier in his lectures about Catholicism. He reported that the Catholic community of his day displayed a "marvelous energy," and Calvinists would do well to recognize that it would "be narrow-minded and short-sighted to underestimate the real power which even now is manifest in Rome's warfare against Atheism and Pantheism." We have to recognize, he told his Princeton audience, that on the present scene "Rome is not an antagonist, but stands on our side." Kuyper testified, "I for my part am not ashamed to confess that on many points my views have been clarified through my study of the Romish theologians."[6]

These are welcome indications that Kuyper would have endorsed Wolters's call for neo-Calvinism to "truly embrace the riches of other traditions, even as it shares its own with others." We can draw even more sustained help in this regard, though, from Bavinck. Kuyper's younger colleague focused throughout his career on the careful development of theological ideas, and did so with a desire to demonstrate at length how an unapologetically Calvinist theologian can engage in charitable engagement with other theological perspectives.

The opportunity for North Americans to learn more from Bavinck than was possible in the past has been greatly enhanced by the recent translation of many of Bavinck's major works into English. Happily, this means that it is no longer possible for English speakers to dismiss Bavinck with faint praise, as did James Hutton Mackay in his 1910 Hastie Lectures in Glasgow when he referred to Bavinck as "Dr. Kuyper's loyal and learned henchman."[7]

Giving and Receiving

In discussing here the evangelical movement's need for a thick theological grounding, I have obviously been complaining about the theological shallowness that I see in much present-day evangelicalism. I want to make it clear, though, that neo-Calvinism also has much to gain by wrestling with these concerns within an evangelical context. On this too, an earlier comment from Al Wolters bears repeating: neo-Calvinists, he observes, have often "paid more attention to the dangers of pietism and its relative neglect of the call to cultural discipleship than to the importance of cultivating genuine piety or authentic spirituality." And he particularly commends, in this regard, the vitality of Pentecostalism.

I can confirm what Wolters observes about the tendency of neo-Calvinists to be quite vocal in our critiques of the dangers of pietism. I have done a bit of this myself. Wolters rightly suggests that this habit brings dangers of its own.

Here too Kuyper himself points us to a more balanced, integrated approach in the large number of devotional pieces he authored over many decades. Clay Cooke and Steve Garber rightly see this significant body of writing as a rich resource for neo-Calvinism:

> The nature of Kuyper's private relationship with God is most lucidly portrayed in his written meditations. These meditations were published weekly for nearly a half-century in the Dutch religious newspaper *De Heraut* (*The Herald*). By inviting people to glimpse his internal life through these intimate writings, Kuyper established an influence that went far beyond the

doctrinal ideas and public positions he is best known for today. Not everyone could grasp the fine points of Kuyper's theology, or all the details of his public speeches, but even the most basic of thinkers could connect with his heartfelt meditations. Consequently, his theological teachings such as "common grace," "antithesis," and "sphere sovereignty" played secondary roles to Kuyper's devotions in rallying people to faithful public action.[8]

A new English-language collection of short (two- to three-page) meditations written by Kuyper in his early years has now joined the collection that has long been in print—so that we now have access to over fifteen hundred pages of Kuyper at his devotional best.[9] These writings can do much to nurture a warmer spirituality into the neo-Calvinist movement—which is certainly a good development in itself, but which can also present neo-Calvinism as more spiritually friendly to the broader evangelical movement.

How Thick?

Back to the question I have been posing to my neo-Calvinist friends: *Do you have to be a Calvinist in order to be a Kuyperian?* Clearly I don't think so—I'm glad Richard Middleton is a Wesleyan Kuyperian. What I still struggle with, though, is the issue of theological sustainability.

Healthy discipleship, including healthy spirituality, requires a solid theological foundation. To say that is not to insist that people who exhibit a healthy faith in their lives must be able to articulate an orthodox foundation for what guides their lives. I like the way that Cooke and Garvey characterized Kuyper's pattern for leading the Calvinist citizenry—those whom he referred to affectionately as *de kleine leyden*, "the little people." He did not expect them to understand the technical details of his theology, but he communicated with them by means of heartfelt meditations, which were themselves expressions of his thick theological convictions. And, having spoken to their hearts, they trusted his uses of sphere sovereignty and the like in exercising his public leadership.

So we see in Kuyper a sound theology giving expression to a deep spirituality that in turn cultivates support for a biblically informed public discipleship. All three are crucial. And while not everyone in the Christian community has to understand the technical theological details, it is important that some members of the community do work at these matters. The broader calling of the Christian community has to be informed by thick theology.

For Kuyper that thickness required careful attention to soteriology, ecclesiology, the doctrines of the covenant, John Calvin's writings, the convictions that were given expression in the Reformed confessions, and so on. Not everyone associated with neo-Calvinism needs to be well-informed about such things. But a healthy neo-Calvinism—or so I am convinced—needs at least some people who commit themselves to thinking carefully about the theological agenda that stimulated and inspired Kuyper to develop his robust theology of culture. To be sure, that agenda was very much shaped by the cultural and theological challenges of the Netherlands in the nineteenth century. But with significant efforts at a careful recontextualization, the insights of that theology can serve as a much-needed resource for the cause of the kingdom in twenty-first-century North America.

The "New Calvinism"

It would be unwise for neo-Calvinists, in our efforts to argue for a specifically Reformed confessional foundation for the Kuyperian themes that we cherish (sphere sovereignty and the like), to fail to learn from those who have been far more successful than we have been in advocating for Calvinism in the North American evangelical context. And yet we—certainly those of us who have drawn directly from the thought of Kuyper, Bavinck, Dooyeweerd, and others in the Dutch tradition—have not been particularly open to that kind of learning.

The persons who might function as our teachers—or at least teaching models—in this regard are the intellectual leaders associated with the movement that *Time* magazine labeled in 2009 "the New Calvinism."[10] The best known of these leaders are Tim Keller, Don Carson, Al Mohler, and John Piper—all of them prominent in The Gospel Coalition organization, which has been widely influential in the younger generation of evangelical students and pastors.

Unfortunately, there has not been any serious dialogue on an ongoing basis between the neo-Calvinists and the New Calvinists. There are complex factors at work in this, and I will not go into them here. One factor that needs to be named, however, has to do with the nature of movements. Specific ideas are associated with gifted leaders who promote those ideas, and persons who are attracted to the ideas frequently link intellectual agreement to personal loyalties. Movements are often sustained by "disciples"—and in movemental terms it is difficult to serve two masters. The fact that different movements might share a significant set of core convictions does not count as much as the matters on which they disagree. And the question of loyalties often comes down to decisions about whose books one will read, whose conferences one will attend, whose podcasts one will listen to.

Someone should write a book on all of that. The reality of differing strands of Calvinism—regularly viewed as competing with one another for movemental loyalties—could be a good place to start. I will not pursue the topic here, except to make some personal comments about how I experience these movemental realities.

I will be candid in offering one case in point. I like much that is associated with The Gospel Coalition (TGC). The organization's "Foundation Documents"—the Confessional Statement and the Theological Vision of Ministry—contain much that not only *could* I sign but would also *like* to sign. What keeps me from actually joining is the strong emphasis on complementarian views regarding issues of gender. But there are also interpersonal factors. Several of TGC's leadership I consider to be good friends. A few others not so—and I know that I bear responsibility for the factors at work in the less-than-friendly relationships.

I will say no more here on that subject, except to express my regret that little dialogue between the New Calvinists and the neo-Calvinists has occurred. From the neo-Calvinist side, I want to go on record as saying that we have much to learn from the New Calvinists.

One learning experience for me has been in reading John Piper's writings. I find much in what he sets forth that is helpful and edifying. There are certain emphases in his writings, though, that have often struck me as incompatible with my own neo-Calvinist convictions. One issue that has loomed large in this regard is the topic that has been a central theme for me in this book: the nature and extent of that in which God delights.

Piper makes much of the fact that God takes delight in his own Being, and that God created us so that we too can take delight in the Being of God.[11] Thus Piper's well-known slight revision of the first question and answer of the Westminster Shorter Catechism: instead of our being created "to glorify God and to enjoy him forever," says Piper, our chief end is to glorify God "*by* enjoying him forever."[12] The plan of redemption is aimed, then, at restoring this human ability in those whom God has elected to eternal life. We are elected to take delight in the God who takes delight in himself.

Piper's formulations here seem to approximate rather closely the case for supralapsarianism set forth by Herman Hoeksema, who portrays God as "the One that is Self-centered and is consecrated to Himself." The Lord, Hoeksema argues, "is attracted by Himself, and He is graciously disposed to Himself. He is charmed by His own loveliness. He delights in His own infinite beauty."[13] The primary—even exclusive—goal of redemptive history, then, is that all who have been elected by God contemplate, and take their supreme pleasure in, the divine holiness.

We get a somewhat different picture from what Herman Bavinck says about the nature of God's delight. For Bavinck the supralapsarian fails to acknowledge that God's "decrees are as abundantly rich in content as the entire history of the world."[14] The cosmos serves, then, as "a suitable theatre for the display, on a creaturely level, of all God's attributes. The world plan is so conceived by God that it can radiantly exhibit his glory and perfections in a manner and measure suited to each creature."[15]

What Bavinck is providing here, of course, is the theological grounding for the neo-Calvinist understanding of common grace. God, says Bavinck, takes delight in his own perfections. But those perfections are on display in God's creation. The created order begins with five "days" of God taking delight in his own perfections as on display in that which God has called into being. God's delight in the Genesis 1 account was not from looking into his own Being but from seeing the perfections of his Being on display in stars, hawks, ocean waves, antelopes, and daisies. And he wants us also to take delight in that display. "The present world, along with its history," says Bavinck, is "an ongoing revelation of God's perfections." And when this present world will be cleansed in the eschaton, the fully restored order of things will "furnish a new humanity with ever new reasons for the worship and glorification of God."[16]

So yes—that looks like a basic contrast to Piper's viewpoint. Piper wants to emphasize the importance of our beholding the glory of God by focusing on the Being of God. For Bavinck, however, our glorifying God includes in great part beholding that which in the creation God takes delight.

The "in great part" clause that I have just used, though, can be a basis for some productive dialogue between Bavinckians and Piperians. Surely we neo-Calvinists should acknowledge that we must also take delight in the very Being of the God who has put his divine perfections on display in the created order. And shouldn't Piper and his friends in turn also allow that the enjoyment of God means not only delighting in God's delight in his own Being but also in taking delight in how God put the perfections of that Being on display in the works of creation—including those products and processes of human culture in which God also takes delight?

Well, in fact, Piper does allow for that. He writes that "Creation is overflow. . . . [It] will show, or display, or communicate God's glory."[17] I think that is a wonderful line. Piper isn't making the panentheistic claim that the creation of finite reality is an inevitable overflow of the divine Being. Rather, it is God's *glory* that flows over into the creation. And we can put the point in Bavinckian terms: the perfections that are contained within God's Being pour into the creation as well and are on display there.

The issues that I have sometimes seen as distancing Piper from Bavinck, then, are not really there as a matter of principle. They have to do with emphases. And I can think of ways in which Piper could expand these emphases in the direction of a more robust theology of culture. But the important point for me here is that we neo-Calvinists can be rightly reminded by Piper that there is a danger of focusing so intently on the divine perfections that are on display in the works of human culture that we miss the necessary grounding of those perfections in the Being of God. A theology of culture needs to stay focused on the *visio dei*. Delight in finite reality should not be divorced from glorifying God by enjoying him in the perfections of his infinite Being.

Dortian Hope[18]

My own appreciation for the basic Calvinist theology of God's sovereign saving grace has been much deepened during the time I have been finishing this book. This has been a period when Calvinists from many nations have been celebrating the four-hundredth anniversary of the great Dordrecht synod that produced the Canons of Dort.

I regularly hear comments within the Reformed world from people who want to distance themselves from the theology of the Canons of Dort. One young pastor put it this way to me by complaining that the canons comprise "a pretty cold and stern document." I disagree. To be sure, one certainly encounters theological sternness in the opening words of the canons: "All men have sinned in Adam, lie under the curse, and are obnoxious to eternal death." That does come across as a rather discouraging opening declaration. The next article however, immediately declares words of hope: "But 'in this the love of God was manifested, that he sent his only begotten Son into the world.'"[19]

Those contrasting themes, stated at the beginning of the canons, capture the heart of Calvinist soteriology: the desperate condition of sinful humankind, cut off from a positive relationship from the Creator by our shared rebellion, and the free and sovereign grace of God who sent the Son into the world.

In proclaiming the divine mercies in that second article, the folks gathered in seventeenth-century Dordrecht obviously had John 3:16 in mind. That verse also informs the neo-Calvinist vision, but—as I have pointed out in an earlier chapter—we like to quote verse 17 as well, pointing out that the Greek word translated as "world" in both verses is *kosmos*, referring to the created order. The great divine love that saves sinners is grounded in a larger love of the whole creation. God does not abandon the fallen creation; instead, he sends the Son to "save" (Greek: *sōthē*) it. And neo-Calvinism insists that the community of those who have been saved by sovereign grace is called to demonstrate God's love for every square of the creation. Thus the movement from the passive—being *acted upon* by sovereign grace—to the active—being *empowered by* that same grace to do God's will as agents of his kingdom.

The canons do not ignore the human agency dimension. They tell us that we "are chosen to faith and the obedience of faith"—God's electing mercy equips us for "the observance of the divine commands."[20] And while there is not any detailed guidance in the canons for this active service, there is an acknowledgment of issues that point us in the direction of common-grace thinking. In unredeemed humanity, the canons say, there are "glimmerings of natural light" that remain after the devastation of the fall into sin. And these "glimmerings" do make possible "some regard for virtue, good order in society, and for maintaining an orderly external deportment."[21]

As Suzanne McDonald has pointed out, this acknowledgment has implications for the active lives of the elect as well. What the canons are saying, she observes, is that "the desire to do what we might call 'civic good' is planted deep in what it means to be human. Unbelievers and believers alike share some sense of right and wrong, and want to at least appear to be doing the right thing." And this means, she continues, that "a shared awareness of injustice can be common ground for Christians and non-Christians as we seek to discern and do what is right."[22]

Neo-Calvinism has rightly insisted that doing what is right encompasses a broad scope—engaging in active cultural discipleship under the lordship of Jesus Christ. But again: this can never be separated from the basic Calvinist message that we are able to serve as agents of Christ's kingdom only because we have been acted upon by the amazing grace of a sovereign God who sustains us—also by grace alone—with power that is necessary for redeemed sinners to walk the paths of discipleship.

17

Divine Generosity

While I sometimes complain about the evangelical tendency to rely heavily on spiritual sound bites as a substitute for good theology, I also know that theological one-liners can on occasion stimulate important insights. One occasion when I realized this was when a Fuller student who had just finished a course that I taught told me that the most important moment in the course for him was my quoting Abraham Kuyper's manifesto— I have made reference to it many times already in this book— that "there is not one square inch of the entire creation about which Jesus Christ does not cry out, 'This is mine! This belongs to me!'"[1] This was not the first time I have heard someone say that discovering that line from Kuyper had a profound influence on how they have come to understand God's purposes in the world.

There have also been moments of my own when a theological one-liner has provided me a significant "Aha!" experience. One of them came from the Japanese-American theologian Kosuke

Koyama when he spoke at a convention of theological educators that I attended. Addressing some basic hermeneutical issues, Koyama said this about the teaching of the rich biblical narrative regarding the character of God: "As we approach the biblical text, each of us has to decide whether the story we encounter on the sacred pages is about a generous God or a stingy God." I quote that line a lot when I teach, and in doing so I make it clear that I vote for divine generosity.

Neo-Calvinism offers a vision of divine generosity, and in doing so it captures a foundational insight of Calvinism as such. Charles Spurgeon nicely summarized the heart of Calvinism in this simple affirmation: "Salvation is of the Lord."[2] This formula rightly emphasizes Calvinism's central focus on salvific concerns. This has to be at the heart of neo-Calvinism as well. The God who takes delight in the richness of creation also takes delight in regenerating the hearts of lost sinners.

Grace: Saving and Common

My *aggiornamento* project in this book would not be complete without doing a little more to update some of my thoughts about saving grace. In my earlier book on common grace, I discuss in the final pages the "wideness in God's mercy." I reject salvific universalism while also resisting "the small number of the elect" theme that we also find in Calvinist teaching. And then I state this: "For all I know—and for all any of us can know—much of what we now think of as common grace may in the end time be revealed to be saving grace."[3]

I wish I had not written that sentence. The paragraph in which it appears would read smoothly without it. More important, though, it is misleading. I know why I wrote it. I meant to acknowledge the need for theological humility in the presence of clear signs of God's generosity. But what I said could be

145

taken as blurring the distinction between common grace and saving grace.

So I must say this in a straightforward manner: I am not a universalist. Indeed, unlike some of my evangelical friends, who say that while they cannot read the Bible as endorsing universalism they do hope it turns out to be true, I am not even tempted by universalism. I like the way N. T. Wright makes the case against universalism. "I find it quite impossible," he writes, "reading the New Testament on the one hand and the newspaper on the other"—he explicitly mentions in this regard reports of "the murder of children and the careless greed that enslaves millions with debts not their own"—"I find it quite impossible . . . to suppose that there will be no ultimate condemnation, no final loss, no human beings to whom, as C. S. Lewis put it, God will eventually say, '*Thy* will be done.'"[4]

Kuyper would not only agree with this but he would do so with theological passion. He was famously intent upon keeping boundary lines clear, and that applies here as well. He was so insistent that we be clear about the difference between saving grace and common grace that he made a point of using two different Dutch words for the two kinds of grace: *genade* for the particular grace that saves and *gratie* for that which simply denoted "favor" with no salvific implications.[5]

Nor was Kuyper content simply to reassure other Calvinists that he was committed to the particularity of electing grace in order to gain their trust on topics related to common grace. Kuyper defended Calvinist soteriology in considerable detail.

This is evident, for example, in his compilation of a series of Sunday pieces that Kuyper published in his newspaper *De Heraut* during 1879–80. Marvin Kamps, who translated them into English, tells us that Kuyper was warned by some of his supporters not to get into debates about controversial issues regarding fine points of the doctrine of election.[6] But Kuyper persisted.

And Kuyper takes the issues on with much passion, appealing to the authority of, among others, Augustine, John Calvin, and the Synod of Dordrecht in making his case for what are commonly referred to these days as "the TULIP doctrines." He frequently bemoans what he sees as theological slippage on these matters in the Reformed community, and he concludes his discussion with a warning that those who dilute Calvinist soteriology run the risk of "cheapen[ing] the honor of the love and mercy of the Lord our God."[7]

I will not get into the details of Kuyper's discussion here. My concern is simply to point to the depth of his convictions on these matters. It is clear that Kuyper, as a champion of the idea of common grace, in no way saw this as incompatible with a passionate defense of Calvinist teachings on God's sovereign grace in bringing sinners to trust in Christ alone for salvation. He clearly believed that common grace was consistent with his views on saving grace. Both sets of teachings were profoundly and integrally expressive of the character of God.

I don't believe that this means that we neo-Calvinists must explicitly link the two in making our case for the basics of Kuyper's theology of culture in a North American context. In this regard it is important to mention an interesting move that Kuyper makes in describing what he sees as the dangerous errors of Arminian theology. He distinguishes between two kinds of people who reject the Calvinist view of electing grace. One is the "dry, moribund, cold intellectual who never gave any evidence of life in his heart," substituting "a lifeless doctrinal skeleton" for "the spiritual, living organism of God's truth."[8] But the other is the kind of Arminian who, in spite of embracing a wrongheaded theology regarding election, nonetheless proclaims the message of "atonement of our sins *through faith in Jesus' blood.*" For that kind of Arminian, says Kuyper, "we have not only no criticism, but from the heart we applaud such preaching."[9] It seems clear that Kuyper would also applaud if such persons combined that kind of preaching with a strong affirmation of common grace as well. He would certainly want to urge them to think differently about some key details in their understanding of the theological basis for their gospel preaching—as will many of us who agree with Kuyper on such matters—but without in any way calling into question their love of the Savior, whose love of sinners is coupled with a love of the whole creation.

Salvific Generosity

While I find Kuyper's 350-page discussion of issues in soteriology theologically clarifying—and even as spiritually edifying—I can understand why several of his supporters urged him not to address the issue. His treatment is clearly polemical in tone, and it is obvious that many in the Reformed circles of his day would feel attacked by him.

Nor is a polemical treatise defending issues relating to limited atonement the kind of work one would recommend to someone who finds Calvinism weak in promoting an understanding of divine generosity. In his opening paragraphs, Kuyper identifies the problem he means to deal with as the claim set forth by a thinker who claimed to be Reformed: "that Christ, according to the purpose and extent of his self-sacrifice, died for all men without exception."[10] Much of his discussion, then, focuses on what Kuyper sees as a too-expansive understanding of the word "all" with reference to how many people God desires to save.

I'm not suggesting here that Kuyper's soteriology is defective. But I am convinced that approaching these matters in a polemical spirit inhibits a full exploration of some aspects of God's saving purposes. Fortunately, we can find helpful resources for that approach in the work of Kuyper's younger associate Herman Bavinck. As I have already noted, Bavinck addressed a broad theological agenda in a careful, systematic manner and with a more moderate spirit than that which typifies Kuyper's polemical writings.

I want to look at Bavinck's efforts to promote a strong sense of divine salvific generosity within a thoroughly orthodox Calvinistic framework. But first I will tell of a personal situation in which Bavinck came to the theological rescue for me.

Concern for Ancestors

The topic of salvific generosity took on a poignancy for me when I was asked for theological counsel by a young Chinese woman. I was lecturing at several "Three Self" theological seminaries in mainland China, and the woman had been assigned to me as my translator. As we reviewed together the contents of the lectures I was going to give, she told me that she had become a Christian only a few years before. She spoke glowingly about having come to a deep faith in Christ after having been raised in a Buddhist family. But she also expressed a sense of inadequacy in her ability to employ theological categories in a sustained manner.

We spent some time talking about what I hoped to get across in my lectures, and then she obviously did an excellent job in translating my lectures—paragraph by paragraph as I delivered them. The inquiries from the audiences in the question-and-answer periods indicated that she had clearly conveyed the theological content of what I had presented.

In my final meeting with her I expressed my gratitude for her efforts. Suddenly her face took on a worried expression, and she said that she needed some theological advice. She was genuinely thrilled to be a Christian, she said, but she was saddened by what her conversion meant for her relationships with her parents. As devout Buddhists they were not hostile to Jesus as such—they saw him as a good ethical teacher. But they were deeply disturbed by the thought that by becoming a Christian their daughter had embraced a religion that condemned all of their ancestors to hell. Through her tears she spoke to me in a pleading tone: "Revering my ancestors means much to me, and I want to assure my parents that I do not want to dishonor my family heritage. So please tell me what I as a Christian can say to my parents about this!"

What immediately came to my mind was a biblical text I had recently been thinking about: the story of the young man whose friends cut a hole in the roof of a home where Jesus was visiting in order to bring their friend to the Savior for healing. I reminded her of the story, and then quoted the response of Jesus in Luke 5:20: "When he saw *their faith*, he said [to the young man], 'Friend, your sins are forgiven you'" (NRSV).

I told her that I found that verse encouraging for her family situation. Jesus healed the young man because of the faith of the man's friends. It may be—and I stressed the word "may"—that there are times when Jesus honors the faith that we manifest on behalf of others who are incapable of having their own faith at that point. It could be, I said, that in her family context the Lord was allowing her faith to count in his dealings with her ancestors. At the very least, I told her, she could tell her parents that she honors her ancestors so much that she fervently prays to the Lord to show mercy to them.

Her face lit up, and she expressed her gratitude. In my own heart, of course, I wondered whether I had gone beyond the boundaries of orthodoxy in my counsel to her. At the same time, however, I was convinced that we Christian theologians cannot avoid wrestling with a topic that takes on urgency in the Asian cultural context.

My conviction about the importance of working on this topic in a serious manner was reinforced in a very helpful way by my reading of an important book by Simon Chan, *Grassroots*

Asian Theology: Thinking the Faith from the Ground Up. Chan, a Pentecostal theologian who is on the faculty at Trinity Theological College in Singapore, is quite critical of the reigning theological methodology among "elite" theologians representing Western ecumenical perspectives. Grassroots Christians in Asia, he argues, have their own profound grasp of their cultural contexts that differs from what is offered by "elite" theologies. These local believers seek out ecclesial communities, typically of a Pentecostal type, in which the actual cultural realities in which they are immersed are taken seriously in the light of the gospel.

Chan explores at some length, for example, the relevance of the kind of honor-and-shame culture that is pervasive in Asia for a Western evangelicalism that has typically concentrated primarily on the concepts of sin and guilt. He does not deny the fact of our guilty sinful condition, but he argues that to fail to pay attention to honor-and-shame themes is to miss much of what the Bible tells us about our shared humanity.

In this regard Chan addresses the topic of the veneration of ancestors, pointing out the same kind of concern that was expressed so earnestly to me by my young Chinese translator. Chan refers specifically to Japanese indigenous Pentecostal movements, where the complaint is regularly raised that traditional Protestant thought has failed to address ancestor veneration. What these local movements have done to remedy this inattention, Chan reports, is to develop a strong emphasis on the communion of the saints, with an expanded sense of continuing relationships between the living and the dead. Furthermore, these movements have instituted "elaborate rituals relating to evangelizing of and communion with the dead," including a "commending of the dead to the mercy of God."[11]

Chan cautiously commends these explorations, pointing to the fact that they are "Christologically grounded" and "sufficiently distinguished from Confucian and Taoist ancestral rites." Furthermore, he says, "when bold steps are taken to find appropriate Christian ritual expressions of ancestral veneration, fresh theological insights have emerged."[12]

Let me make it clear that I am not agreeing here with Chan's favorable assessment of these developments, even in the cautious form in which he offers it. But I do want to point out that the practices he describes can be thought about in relationship to key neo-Calvinist themes. Chan observes, for example, that the deep commitment to "ancestor veneration underscores the unsurpassed value placed on the family in Asia."[13] It has to do, then, with a theological focus on the sphere of the family, emphasizing our obligation to attend more carefully to these concerns than we Calvinists have engaged in thus far. We owe that hard theological work to those who have already come to a saving knowledge of Jesus Christ in contexts where ancestral veneration is so deeply embedded in the important creational sphere of family life. And, I should add, we owe it also to our own cultural settings, where many new questions are being raised about the nature of family and marriage.

Help from Herman Bavinck

Here is where I have found Bavinck to be particularly helpful. On the subject of the salvific status of those who have not heard the gospel proclaimed, Bavinck leaves considerable room for mystery. "In light of Scripture," he writes, "both with regard to the salvation of pagans and that of children who die in infancy, we cannot get beyond abstaining from a firm judgment, in either a positive or a negative sense." Then Bavinck appeals nicely to historic Calvinism by quoting from the Westminster Confession's chapter "Of Effectual Calling": "Elect infants, dying in infancy, are regenerated and saved by Christ through the Spirit, who worketh when, and where, and how he pleaseth. So also are all other elect persons who are incapable of being outwardly called by the ministry of the Word."[14] Bavinck drew particular attention—and with obvious theological approval—to the final clause, stating that in addition to children who die in infancy there are others who, while not capable of being "outwardly called by the ministry of the Word," are nonetheless recipients of electing grace of the God who works when, and where, and how he pleases.

Bavinck's use of the Westminster article to allow for some Calvinist flexibility in understanding God's salvific dealings with sinful human beings gives me some reassurance regarding my counsel to my Chinese translator. His refusal to operate with rigid categories in this area is also evident in his critique of what he labels the "single decree" understanding of reprobation in the supralapsarian strand of Calvinism. It is not theologically proper, Bavinck insists, "to say that in the eternal state of the lost, God *exclusively* reveals his justice, and that in that of the elect he *exclusively* reveals his mercy. Also in the church purchased as it was by the blood of his Son, God's justice becomes manifest." Then he immediately adds this verdict: "And also in the place of perdition there are degrees of punishment and glimmerings of his mercy."[15] And lest we miss the point he is making in saying that, he repeats it three pages later: "It is not true that God's justice can only be manifested in the wretched state of the lost and his mercy only in the blessedness of the elect, for in heaven, too, his justice and holiness are radiantly present, and even in hell there is still some evidence of his mercy and goodness."[16]

I see these Bavinckian comments more as theological hints than as clear doctrinal formulations. But they are *good* hints—reassuring to those of us who, while firmly rejecting universalism, want to cultivate a more generous understanding of sovereign saving grace than is often on display among Calvinists.

No Calvinist can entertain the notion that people can be saved apart from the atoning work of Jesus Christ that was completed at Calvary. But neither should any Calvinist complain about some element of mystery in our understanding of how God applies the merits of Christ to individual lives—and to the cosmos that the Savior also came to rescue from the curse of sin.

In my efforts to make a case for neo-Calvinism, I have often focused on the active dimensions of the Christian life. I emphasize the way in which Calvinist soteriology makes primary theological use of the passive voice, and I have done so here as well. We are totally incapable of initiating or contributing to our salvation. We are *acted upon* by God. He elects us. He plants the seeds of regeneration in our hearts. He holds us with a love that will not let us go.

The God of the Bible "works when, and where, and how he pleases." In declaring this the Westminster divines were rightly reminding us that there is much about his electing purposes that is hidden from us. This same sense of humility in the face of the divine mysteries made Deuteronomy 29:29 a favorite verse of many Calvinists in the past, and it is one of my favorites also: "The secret things belong unto the LORD our God: but those things which are revealed belong unto us and to our children for ever, that we may do all the words of this law" (KJV).

Fortunately, not all of what pleases the Lord remains hidden from us. He has revealed some important things in his Word about what gives him delight. He certainly takes delight in the salvation of sinners, and he calls them to share in the ways in which he takes delight in stars and ponds and wild goats. And—I have been arguing in these pages—he wants us to join him in delighting in well-crafted Chinese vases and in nicely written paragraphs by Scottish satirists.

I have made much in this book about the need for active cultural engagement in our efforts to please the Lord. In endorsing the strong passive themes in Calvinist soteriology—that in saving us, God does *for* us and *to* us what we could never do for ourselves—I have observed that neo-Calvinism takes the next theological step: having saved us by sovereign grace, God *empowers* us for active service. We are incorporated into the life of a people—a covenant community—who must bear witness in our words and deeds to Christ's rule over all the square inches of the cosmos.

In concluding here, though, it is good to give Kuyper the last word. As he ended his Stone Lectures, he turned to a passive image, citing for his Princeton audience the example of the ancient aeolian harp, a stringed instrument that the Greeks would hang in an open window. The strings were tuned in such a way that they would produce harmonic sounds when Aeolus, the God of the winds, sent breezes their way.

If Calvinists are to experience the renewal that can make us effective agents of renewal in a time of widespread unbelief, said Kuyper, we must "be nothing but such an Aeolian Harp—absolutely powerless, as it is, without the quickening Spirit of God." This means, he pleaded, that we must "feel it our God-given duty to keep our harp, its strings tuned aright, ready in the window of God's Holy Zion, awaiting the breath of the Spirit."[17]

Kuyper was telling nineteenth-century Calvinists that in order to serve the Lord properly, they had to stay tuned to the empowering presence of the Spirit of the living God. That is a profound word for twenty-first-century Calvinists as well.

Notes

Introduction

1. Abraham Kuyper, *Lectures on Calvinism* (Grand Rapids: Eerdmans, 1931), 41.

2. Paul Gutjahr, *Charles Hodge: Guardian of American Orthodoxy* (New York: Oxford University Press, 2011), 363.

3. Al Wolters, *Creation Regained: Biblical Basics for a Reformational Worldview* (Grand Rapids: Eerdmans, 2005).

4. Craig G. Bartholomew, *Contours of the Kuyperian Tradition: A Systematic Introduction*, 2nd ed. (Downers Grove, IL: IVP Academic, 2017).

5. Jochem Douma, *Common Grace in Kuyper, Schilder, and Calvin: Exposition, Comparison, and Evaluation*, ed. William Helder, trans. Albert H. Oosterhoff (Hamilton, ON: Lucerna CRTS, 2017).

Chapter 1 God's Complex Concerns

1. Richard J. Mouw, *Uncommon Decency: Christian Civility in an Uncivil World*, 2nd ed. (Downers Grove, IL: InterVarsity, 2010), 159–69.

2. Abraham Kuyper, *Christianity and the Class Struggle*, trans. Dirk Jellema (Grand Rapids: Piet Heyn, 1950), 27–28.

Chapter 2 The Joys of Discipleship

1. See Kierkegaard's meditation, "The Joy in the Thought That It Is Not the Way Which Is Narrow, but the Narrowness Which Is the Way," in Søren Kierkegaard, *Edifying Discourses: A Selection*, edited by Paul L. Holmer, translated by David F. and Lillian Marvin Swenson (New York: Harper and Brothers, 1958), 209–29.

2. John H. Yoder, *The Politics of Jesus: Vicit Agnus Noster* (Grand Rapids: Eerdmans, 1972), 97.

3. Dietrich Bonhoeffer, *The Cost of Discipleship* (New York: Touchstone Books, 1995), 37.

4. Bonhoeffer, *Cost of Discipleship*, 38.

5. Bonhoeffer, *Cost of Discipleship*, 297.

Chapter 3 The Divine Distance

1. Andrew Greeley, *The Catholic Imagination* (Oakland: University of California Press, 2000), 163.

2. Greeley, *Catholic Imagination*, 5.

3. Cornelius Van Til, *Common Grace* (Philadelphia: P&R, 1954), 9.

4. Karl Rahner, *Foundations of Christian Faith: An Introduction to the Idea of Christianity* (New York: Crossroad, 2002), 200–202.

5. Klaas Schilder, *Heidlerbergsche Catechismus* (Goes, Netherlands: Oosterbaan & Le Cointre, 1949), 2:93, quoted in Jelle Faber, *Essays in Reformed Doctrine* (Neerlandia, AB: Inheritance Publications, 1990), 51.

6. *The Heidelberg Catechism*, questions and answers 47 and 49, in Philip Schaff, *The Creeds of Christendom* (Grand Rapids: Baker, 1996), 3:322–23.

7. See Richard J. Mouw, "My Favorite Heretic," *First Things*, Sept. 16, 2014, https://www.firstthings.com/web-exclusives/2014/09/my-favorite-heretic.

8. Janice Knight, *Orthodoxies in Massachusetts: Rereading American Puritanism* (Cambridge, MA: Harvard University Press, 1994), 78.

9. Knight, *Orthodoxies in Massachusetts*, 77.

10. Richard Sibbes, *The Complete Works of Richard Sibbes* (Edinburgh: J. Nichol, 1862–1864), 4:196, quoted in Knight, *Orthodoxies in Massachusetts*, 83.

Chapter 4 "That's Good!"

1. Lewis B. Smedes, *My God and I: A Spiritual Memoir* (Grand Rapids: Eerdmans, 2003), 56–57.

2. Abraham Kuyper, "Sphere Sovereignty," in *Abraham Kuyper: A Centennial Reader*, ed. James D. Bratt (Grand Rapids: Eerdmans, 1998), 488.

3. G. K. Chesterton, *Orthodoxy* (Garden City, NY: Doubleday, 1959), 60.

4. Herman Bavinck, *Reformed Dogmatics*, vol. 2, *God and Creation*, ed. John Bolt, trans. John Vriend (Grand Rapids: Baker Academic, 2004), 391–92.

Chapter 5 Assessing the Natural Mind

1. Richard J. Mouw, *Adventures in Evangelical Civility: A Lifelong Quest for Common Ground* (Grand Rapids: Brazos, 2016), 7–12.

2. Cornelius Van Til, *Common Grace and Witness-Bearing* (Philadelphia: P&R, 1956), 72.

3. Van Til, *Common Grace and Witness-Bearing*, 85.

4. Van Til, *Common Grace and Witness-Bearing*, 82–83.

5. Van Til, *Common Grace and Witness-Bearing*, 57.

6. Van Til, *Common Grace and Witness-Bearing*, 40.

7. Van Til, *Common Grace and Witness-Bearing*, 7.

8. Van Til, *Common Grace and Witness-Bearing*, 30 (emphasis in original).

9. Van Til, *Common Grace and Witness-Bearing*, 92.

10. Van Til, *Common Grace and Witness-Bearing*, 44.

11. Van Til, *Common Grace and Witness-Bearing*, 85.

Chapter 6 Is "Restraint" Enough?

1. Cornelius Van Til, *Common Grace* (Philadelphia: P&R, 1954), 43–44.

2. Daniel Strange, *Their Rock Is Not Like Our Rock: A Theology of Religions* (Grand Rapids: Zondervan, 2014), 246.

3. St. Augustine, *On Christian Doctrine, in Four Books*, trans. James Shaw, chap. 40, no. 60, http://www.ccel.org/ccel/augustine/doctrine.xli.html.

4. St. Augustine, *On Christian Doctrine*, chap. 40, no. 60.

5. Thomas Carlyle, *Sartor Resartus* (Oxford: Oxford University Press, 1987), 3.

6. The account of the debates leading up to the 1924 affirmation of common grace, and the subsequent developments leading to the departure of the Hoeksema group, is given in detail in Herman Hoeksema, *The Protestant Reformed Churches in America: Their Origin, Early History and Doctrine* (Grand Rapids: First Protestant Reformed Church, 1936).

7. Van Til provides the official text of these three points in *Common Grace*, 19–22.

8. Herman Hoeksema, *The Protestant Reformed Churches in America: Their Origins, Early History, and Doctrine* (Grand Rapids: First Protestant Reformed Church, 1936), 320.

9. Herman Hoeksema, *A Triple Breach: In the Foundation of the Reformed Truth* (Grandville, MI: The Evangelism Committee of Southwest Protestant Reformed Church, 1992), 68.

Chapter 7 A Pause for Some "Meta-Calvinist" Considerations

1. David Engelsma, *Common Grace Revisited: In Response to Richard J. Mouw's* He Shines in All That's Fair (Grandville, MI: Reformed Free Publishing Association, 2003), 41.

2. Richard J. Mouw, *He Shines in All That's Fair: Culture and Common Grace* (Grand Rapids: Eerdmans, 2001), 41–42.

3. Engelsma, *Common Grace Revisited*, 43 (emphasis in original).

4. Engelsma, *Common Grace Revisited*, 34.

5. Engelsma, *Common Grace Revisited*, 45.

6. Engelsma, *Common Grace Revisited*, 94.

7. John Calvin, *Institutes of the Christian Religion*, ed. John T. McNeill, trans. Ford Lewis Battles (Philadelphia: Westminster Press, 1960), 2.3.6, p. 273.

8. Calvin, *Institutes* 2.2.14, p. 273.

9. Engelsma, *Common Grace Revisited*, 45.

10. Abraham Kuyper, *Common Grace: God's Gifts for a Fallen World*, 3 vols., trans. Nelson D. Kloosterman and Ed M. van der Maas (Bellingham, WA: Lexham Press, 2019), 2:59.

11. Kuyper, *Common Grace*, 2:58–59.

12. Kuyper, *Common Grace*, 1:539–40.

13. Alasdair MacIntyre, *After Virtue: A Study in Moral Theory* (Notre Dame, IN: University of Notre Dame Press, 1981), 22.

14. Calvin's public leadership in Geneva has been well documented. My favorite book on the subject is W. Fred Graham, *The Constructive Revolutionary: John Calvin and His Socio-Economic Impact* (Richmond: John Knox, 1971).

15. Calvin, *Institutes* 2.8.54–55, pp. 417–19 (emphasis added).

16. Charles Spurgeon, quoted in Iain H. Murray, *Spurgeon v. Hyper-Calvinism: The Battle for Gospel Preaching* (Edinburgh: Banner of Truth, 1995), 76.

17. The debate is transcribed at http://www.prca.org/current/Articles/a%20 debate%20on%20common%20grace%20-%20engelsma-mouw.htm.

Chapter 8 Resisting an Altar Call

1. James K. A. Smith, *How (Not) to be Secular: Reading Charles Taylor* (Grand Rapids: Eerdmans, 2014).

2. James K. A. Smith, *You Are What You Love: The Spiritual Power of Habit* (Grand Rapids: Brazos, 2016).

3. James K. A. Smith, *Awaiting the King: Reforming Public Theology* (Grand Rapids: Baker Academic, 2017), xi.

4. Smith, *Awaiting the King*, xii.

5. Smith, *Awaiting the King*, 123.

6. Smith, *Awaiting the King*, 124 (emphasis in original).

7. Richard J. Mouw and John H. Yoder, "Evangelical Ethics and the Anabaptist-Reformed Dialogue," *The Journal of Religious Ethics* 17 (Fall 1989): 121–37.

8. Don Richardson, *Eternity in Their Hearts* (Minneapolis: Bethany House, 2006), 84.

9. Abraham Kuyper, *Common Grace: God's Gifts for a Fallen World*, 3 vols., trans. Nelson D. Kloosterman and Ed M. van der Maas (Bellingham, WA: Lexham Press, 2019), 1:539–40.

10. John Calvin, *Institutes of the Christian Religion*, ed. John T. McNeill, trans. Ford Lewis Battles (Philadelphia: Westminster Press, 1960), 2.3.3, p. 292.

11. Calvin, *Institutes* 2.3.4, p. 393.

12. Calvin, *Institutes* 2.3.4, p. 294.

13. Herman Bavinck, "Calvin and Common Grace," trans. Geerhardus Vos, *The Princeton Theological Review* 7, no. 3 (1909): 454.

14. Bavinck, "Calvin and Common Grace," 455.

15. Canons of the Synod of Dort, heads 3 and 4, art. 16, in Philip Schaff, *The Creeds of Christendom* (Grand Rapids: Baker, 1996), 3:591.

Chapter 9 A Shared Humanness

1. Abraham Kuyper, *The Work of the Holy Spirit*, trans. Henri DeVries (Grand Rapids: Eerdmans, 1946), 645 (emphasis added).

2. Abraham Kuyper, *Common Grace: God's Gifts for a Fallen World*, 3 vols., trans. Nelson D. Kloosterman and Ed M. van der Maas (Bellingham, WA: Lexham Press, 2019), 2:59.

3. Henry Stob, *Theological Reflections* (Grand Rapids: Eerdmans, 1982), 243.

4. Stob, *Theological Reflections*, 248.

5. Kuyper, *Work of the Holy Spirit*, 645–46 (emphasis added).

6. Abraham Kuyper, *Christianity and the Class Struggle*, trans. Dirk Jellema (Grand Rapids: Piet Heyn, 1950), 27–28 (emphasis added).

7. Kuyper, *Work of the Holy Spirit*, 551.

8. *Gaudiam et Spes*, Promulgated by His Holiness, Pope Paul VI, on December 7, 1965, http://www.vatican.va/archive/hist_councils/ii_vatican_council/documents/vat-ii_cons_19651207_gaudium-et-spes_en.html.

Chapter 10 The Larger Story

1. This, of course, is the well-known response to the question regarding the chief end of humanity in the Westminster Shorter Catechism, question and answer 1, in Philip Schaff, *The Creeds of Christendom* (Grand Rapids: Baker, 1996), 3:676.

2. Jochem Douma, *Common Grace in Kuyper, Schilder, and Calvin: Exposition, Comparison, and Evaluation*, ed. William Helder, trans. Albert H. Oosterhoff (Hamilton, ON: Lucerna CRTS, 2017), 298.

3. Richard J. Mouw, *When the Kings Come Marching In*, rev. ed. (Grand Rapids: Eerdmans, 2002).

4. Herman Bavinck, *Reformed Dogmatics*, vol. 2, *God and Creation*, ed. John Bolt, trans. John Vriend (Grand Rapids: Baker Academic, 2004), 577–78.

5. Bavinck, *Reformed Dogmatics*, 2:577–78.

6. Herman Bavinck, *Reformed Dogmatics*, vol. 4, *Holy Spirit, Church, and New Creation*, ed. John Bolt, trans. John Vriend (Grand Rapids: Baker Academic, 2008), 727.

Chapter 11 But Is It "Grace"?

1. Christine Pohl, *Making Room: Recovering Hospitality as a Christian Tradition* (Grand Rapids: Eerdmans, 1999).

2. Pohl, *Making Room*, 4.

3. Henry R. Van Til, *The Calvinistic Concept of Culture* (Grand Rapids: Baker, 1959), 244.

4. Richard J. Mouw, *He Shines in All That's Fair: Culture and Common Grace* (Grand Rapids: Eerdmans, 2001), 49.

5. Jochem Douma, *Common Grace in Kuyper, Schilder, and Calvin: Exposition, Comparison, and Evaluation*, ed. William Helder, trans. Albert H. Oosterhoff (Hamilton, ON: Lucerna CRTS, 2017), 247.

6. Douma, *Common Grace*, 247–48.

7. Douma, *Common Grace*, 248.

8. Georges Bernanos, *Diary of a Country Priest* (New York: Carroll and Graf, 1989), 298.

Chapter 12 Attending to the Antithesis

1. James Bratt, *Dutch Calvinism in Modern America* (Grand Rapids: Eerdmans, 1984), 50.

2. Bratt, *Dutch Calvinism*, 51.

3. Bratt, *Dutch Calvinism*, 52.

4. Belgic Confession, art. 37, in Philip Schaff, *The Creeds of Christendom* (Grand Rapids: Baker, 1996), 3:436.

5. Lesslie Newbigin, *Foolishness to the Greeks* (Grand Rapids: Eerdmans, 2006), 136.

6. Quirinus Breen, *Christianity and Humanism: Studies in the History of Ideas* (Grand Rapids: Eerdmans, 1968), 257.

7. Henry Stob, *Theological Reflections* (Grand Rapids: Eerdmans, 1982), 243.

Chapter 13   Religions Now "More Precisely Known"

1. Herman Bavinck, *Reformed Dogmatics*, vol. 1, *Prolegomena*, ed. John Bolt, trans. John Vriend (Grand Rapids: Baker Academic, 2003), 318.

2. Jochem Douma, *Common Grace in Kuyper, Schilder, and Calvin: Exposition, Comparison, and Evaluation*, ed. William Helder, trans. Albert H. Oosterhoff (Hamilton, ON: Lucerna CRTS, 2017), 251–55.

3. Philip Schaff, *The Creeds of Christendom* (Grand Rapids: Baker, 1996), 3:384, 600.

4. Abraham Kuyper, *On Islam*, trans. Jan van Vliet (Bellingham, WA: Lexham Press, 2017) 167.

5. Kuyper, *On Islam*, 168.

6. Kuyper, *On Islam*, 168.

7. John Stanley's essay, "Antithesis, Common Grace, and the 'Reciprocity of Transformation': Towards a Distinctively Neo-Calvinist *Theologia Religionum* for Our Time," is a working paper based on his dissertation research. I am quoting from it with his permission.

8. Sander Griffioen and Richard Mouw, *Pluralisms and Horizons: An Essay in Christian Public Philosophy* (Grand Rapids: Eerdmans, 1993).

9. Cornelis van der Kooi, "Towards an Abrahamic Ecumenism? The Search for the Universality of the Divine Mystery," *Acta Theologica* 32, no. 2 (December 2012), 248–52.

10. Abraham Kuyper, *Women of the Old Testament*, trans. Henry Zylstra (Grand Rapids: Zondervan, 1934), 5.

11. Kuyper, *Women of the Old Testament*, 18–19.

Chapter 14   Common Grace and "the Last Days"

1. Stanley Hauerwas, *The Peaceable Kingdom: A Primer in Social Ethics* (Notre Dame, IN: University of Notre Dame Press, 1983), 99.

2. Hauerwas, *Peaceable Kingdom*, 100.

3. Klaas Schilder, *Christ and Culture*, trans. William Helder and Albert H. Oosterhoff (Hamilton, ON: Lucerna CRTS, 2016), 135.

4. Schilder, *Christ and Culture*, 105.

5. N. H. Gootjes, "Schilder on Christ and Culture," in *Always Obedient: Essays on the Teachings of Dr. Klaas Schilder*, ed. J. Geertsema (Phillipsburg, NJ: P&R, 1995), 35.

6. Schilder, *Christ and Culture*, 132.

7. Schilder, *Christ and Culture*, 137.

8. Schilder, *Christ and Culture*, 139.

9. Schilder, *Christ and Culture*, 139.

10. Schilder, *Christ and Culture*, 140.

11. Schilder, *Christ and Culture*, 114.

12. Schilder, *Christ and Culture*, 138, 140.

13. Jochem Douma, *Common Grace in Kuyper, Schilder, and Calvin: Exposition, Comparison, and Evaluation*, ed. William Helder, trans. Albert H. Oosterhoff (Hamilton, ON: Lucerna CRTS, 2017), 292 (emphasis in original).

14. Schilder, *Christ and Culture*, 114–15.

15. Abraham Kuyper, *Common Grace: God's Gifts for a Fallen World*, 3 vols., trans. Nelson D. Kloosterman and Ed M. van der Maas (Bellingham, WA: Lexham Press, 2019), 1:516–17.

16. Kuyper, *Common Grace*, 1:523.

17. Abraham Kuyper, *Lectures on Calvinism* (Grand Rapids: Eerdmans, 1931), 71–72.

18. Gordon J. Spykman, *Reformational Theology: A New Paradigm for Doing Dogmatics* (Grand Rapids: Eerdmans, 1992), 180.

19. Herman Dooyeweerd, *A New Critique of Theoretical Thought*, vol. 1, *The Necessary Presuppositions of Philosophy*, trans. D. H. Freedman and William Young (Philadelphia: P&R, 1953), 99n1.

20. Schilder, *Christ and Culture*, 113.

21. Schilder, *Christ and Culture*, 57.

22. Kuyper, *Common Grace*, 1:526.

23. Kuyper, *Common Grace*, 1:529.

24. Kuyper, *Common Grace*, 1:532.

25. Kuyper, *Common Grace*, 1:533.

26. Schilder, *Christ and Culture*, 16–17.

27. Cf. "Some Reflections on Sphere Sovereignty," in Richard J. Mouw, *The Challenges of Cultural Discipleship: Essays in the Line of Abraham Kuyper* (Grand Rapids: Eerdmans, 2012), esp. 43–46.

28. I refer here to my book, *Adventures in Christian Civility: A Lifelong Quest for Common Ground* (Grand Rapids: Brazos, 2016).

29. Kuyper, *Common Grace*, 1:533.

Chapter 15 Neo-Calvinism in America

1. Abraham Kuyper, *Lectures on Calvinism* (Grand Rapids: Eerdmans, 1931), 9.

2. George Harinck, "A Triumphal Procession?," in *Kuyper Reconsidered: Aspects of His Life and Work*, ed. Cornelis van der Kooi and Jan de Bruijn (Amsterdam: VU Uitgeverij, 1999), 276.

3. Harinck, "Triumphal Procession?," 275–77.

4. Harinck, "Triumphal Procession?," 277.

5. James Bratt, *Dutch Calvinism in Modern America* (Grand Rapids: Eerdmans, 1984), 93–122.

6. Henry Stob, *Theological Reflections* (Grand Rapids: Eerdmans, 1982), 187–94.

7. Harinck, "Triumphal Procession?," 278.

8. Byron Borger, "My Big Back Story and a Sale on Kuyperian Books from the 'Full Bodied Community' Event in Pittsburgh," *Booknotes* (blog), November 14, 2017, https://www.heartsandmindsbooks.com/2017/11/my-big-back-story-and-a-sale-on-kuyperian-books-from-the-full-bodied-community-event-in-pittsburgh.

9. Al Wolters, "What Is to Be Done . . . Toward a Neo-Calvinist Agenda?," *Comment* 23, no. 2 (December 2005): 38.

10. Henry Zwaanstra, *Reformed Thought and Experience in a New World: A Study of the Christian Reformed Church and Its American Environment, 1890–1918* (Kampen, Netherlands: Kok, 1973), 31, 42–52.

Chapter 16 How Much Calvinism?

1. Al Wolters, "What Is to Be Done . . . Toward a Neo-Calvinist Agenda?," *Comment* 23, no. 2 (December 2005): 39.

2. Wolters, "What Is to Be Done?," 40.

3. Wolters, "What Is to Be Done?," 41.

4. David W. Bebbington, *Evangelicalism in Modern Britain: A History from the 1730s to the 1980s* (London: Unwin Hyman, 1989), 2–17.

5. Abraham Kuyper, *Lectures on Calvinism* (Grand Rapids: Eerdmans, 1931), 181.

6. Kuyper, *Lectures on Calvinism*, 183–84.

7. James Hutton Mackay, *Religious Thought in Holland in the Nineteenth Century* (London: Hodder and Stoughton, 1981), x–xi.

8. Clay Cooke and Steven Garber, "Kuyper the Mystic: Private Piety and Public Life," *Comment* 2 (Summer 2010): 25.

9. A large collection of Kuyper's meditations was translated into English by John Hendrik De Vries in 1924 as *To Be Near Unto God* and has remained in print ever since in various formats and editions. The more recent collection, translated by James De Jong, is *Honey from the Rock: Daily Devotions from Young Kuyper* (Bellingham, WA: Lexham Press, 2018).

10. David Van Bierma, "The New Calvinism," *Time*, March 12, 2009, http://content.time.com/time/specials/packages/article/0,28804,1884779_1884782_1884760,00.html.

11. John Piper, *The Pleasures of God: Meditations on God's Delight in Being God*, rev. and expanded ed. (Portland, OR: Multnomah, 2012).

12. John Piper, *Desiring God: Meditations of a Christian Hedonist* (Portland, OR: Multnomah, 1986), 19.

13. Herman Hoeksema, *Reformed Dogmatics*, vol. 1, 2nd ed. (Grandville, MI: Reformed Free Publishing Association, 2004), 160.

14. Herman Bavinck, *Reformed Dogmatics*, vol. 2, *God and Creation*, ed. John Bolt, trans. John Vriend (Grand Rapids: Baker Academic, 2004), 390.

15. Bavinck, *Reformed Dogmatics*, 2:373.

16. Bavinck, *Reformed Dogmatics*, 2:392.

17. John Piper, *Reading the Bible Supernaturally: Seeing and Savoring the Glory of God in Scripture* (Wheaton: Crossway, 2017), 47.

18. In this section I am drawing on my plenary address commemorating the four-hundredth anniversary of the Synod of Dort, given at Dordrecht, the

Netherlands, on November 16, 2018, and published as Richard J. Mouw, "The Worldview of the Synod of Dort," *Kerk en Theologie* 70, no. 1 (January 2019): 17–24.

19. The Canons of the Synod of Dort, head 1, art. 9, in Philip Schaff, *The Creeds of Christendom* (Grand Rapids: Baker, 1996), 3:581.

20. Canons of the Synod of Dort, head 1, art. 9, in Schaff, *Creeds* 3:583.

21. Canons of the Synod of Dort, heads 3 and 4, art. 4, in Schaff, *Creeds*, 3:588.

22. Suzanne McDonald, "The Canons of Dort: No Line between 'Deserving' and 'Undeserving,'" *Do Justice*, October 12, 2017, http://dojustice.crcna.org/article /canons-dort-no-line-between-deserving-and-undeserving.

Chapter 17 Divine Generosity

1. Abraham Kuyper, "Sphere Sovereignty," in *Abraham Kuyper: A Centennial Reader*, ed. James D. Bratt (Grand Rapids: Eerdmans, 1998), 488.

2. Charles Spurgeon, "A Defense of Calvinism," https://archive.spurgeon.org /calvinis.php.

3. Richard J. Mouw, *He Shines in All That's Fair: Culture and Common Grace* (Grand Rapids: Eerdmans, 2001), 100.

4. N. T. Wright, *Surprised by Hope: Rethinking Heaven, the Resurrection, and the Mission of the Church* (New York: HarperOne, 2008), 182–83.

5. Kuyper explains this in "Why the Term 'Common' Grace?," which is an appendix to *Common Grace: God's Gifts for a Fallen World*, 3 vols., trans. Nelson D. Kloosterman and Ed M. van der Maas (Bellingham, WA: Lexham Press, 2019), 1:596–98.

6. Marvin Kamps, translator's introduction to Abraham Kuyper, *Particular Grace: A Defense of God's Sovereignty in Salvation* (Grandville, MI: Reformed Free Publishing Association, 2001), ix.

7. Kuyper, *Particular Grace*, 350.

8. Kuyper, *Particular Grace*, 65.

9. Kuyper, *Particular Grace*, 18 (emphasis in original).

10. Kuyper, *Particular Grace*, 3.

11. Simon Chan, *Grassroots Asian Theology: Thinking the Faith from the Ground Up* (Downers Grove, IL: IVP Academic, 2014), 193–94.

12. Chan, *Grassroots Asian Theology*, 202.

13. Chan, *Grassroots Asian Theology*, 189.

14. Herman Bavinck, *Reformed Dogmatics*, vol. 4, *Holy Spirit, Church, and New Creation* (Grand Rapids: Baker Academic, 2008), 726.

15. Herman Bavinck, *Reformed Dogmatics*, vol. 2, *God and Creation* (Grand Rapids: Baker Academic, 2004), 386.

16. Bavinck, *Reformed Dogmatics*, 2:389.

17. Abraham Kuyper, *Lectures on Calvinism* (Grand Rapids: Eerdmans, 1931), 199.